EDITH WHARTON
A Critical Interpretation

Also by Geoffrey Walton

Metaphysical to Augustan

EDITH WHARTON
A Critical Interpretation

SECOND EDITION, REVISED

GEOFFREY WALTON

Rutherford • Madison • Teaneck
FAIRLEIGH DICKINSON UNIVERSITY PRESS
London • Toronto
ASSOCIATED UNIVERSITY PRESSES

© 1970, 1982 by Geoffrey Walton

Associated University Presses, Inc.
4 Cornwall Drive
East Brunswick, NJ 08816

Associated University Presses Ltd
27 Chancery Lane
London WC2A 1NF, England

Associated University Presses
Toronto M5E 1A7, Canada

Library of Congress Cataloging in Publication Data

Walton, Geoffrey.
  Edith, Wharton, a critical interpretation.

  Bibliography: p.
  Includes index.
  1. Wharton, Edith, 1862–1937—Criticism and
interpretation.   I. Title.
  PS3545.H16Z9   1983   813'.52   82-2413
  ISBN 0-8386-3164-9   AACR2

Printed in the United States of America

Contents

Preface to the Second Edition

When I first read the novels of Edith Wharton in the fifties and sixties, interest in her work was at a low ebb. Her books were out of print in Britain, and I believe that not many of them were available new in the United States. However, I managed to pick up almost all of them second-hand (in first editions!) over here for a few shillings each, which was, of course, an indication of public indifference.

There has been a change of attitude to her in her own country since then but not as much as there should have been in Britain. Owing no doubt to the mixed quality of her later work combined with the common fate of writers who live on into a new epoch—in her case across a social and cultural revolution—with which they are not in sympathy, Edith Wharton's fiction suffered more than the usual revulsion of taste that befalls almost every writer late in life or soon after death. As a start of a revival Q. D. Leavis contributed a discriminatingly laudatory article to *Scrutiny*[1] in 1938, though she unfortunately made merely passing mention of *The Buccaneers*, the publication of which was the immediate reason for her study. But the war soon supervened, and the postwar reprintings, grateful as one was for them, did not proceed very far in Britain. Percy Lubbock's personal tribute, *Portrait of Edith Wharton* (1947), was what

---

1. "Henry James's Heiress," *Scrutiny* 7, December, 1938, reprinted in *Edith Wharton*, ed. I. Howe, New York: Prentice Hall, 1962.

its title suggests and not a critical account of her work.

After her tremendous reputation in the first two decades of the century in America and her perhaps rather more honorary status in the interwar years, admiration for Edith Wharton as a novelist seems, however, to have been rather uncertain in America also. Edmund Wilson[2] did her less than justice a year after her death, and, so far from time's improving the critical focus, Van Wyck Brooks,[3] for example, shows less understanding of her work than did Henry Dwight Sedgwick[4] or R. M. Lovett[5] writing in her lifetime. Mrs. Wharton herself said in her autobiography, *A Backward Glance,* that members of her social class "were the heirs of an old tradition of European culture which the country [had by then] totally rejected." Whether this is true or not, it seems that her work is so widely different from what was being established during those years as the mainstream of American literature that the recognition accorded to her, even when enthusiastic, was and still is sometimes disappointing in quality. However, Blake Nevius,[6] shortly after the war, drew attention to Edith Wharton as not only Henry James's heiress but also, though one may disagree with some of his analyses, as a great novelist of manners in her own right. Irving Howe's anthology of criticism[7] contains worthy material, especially his own contributions, and Louis Auchincloss[8] has continued the process of readjusting the balance of taste in her favor. She seems to be at last

---

2. "Justice to Edith Wharton," *New Republic,* 29 June, 1938, reprinted in *The Wound and the Bow,* London: Secker, 1941.

3. *The Confident Years,* New York: Dutton, 1952, chapter XVI.

4. "Mrs. Wharton," *The New American Type and Other Essays,* Boston: Houghton Mifflin, 1908.

5. *Edith Wharton,* New York: McBride, 1925.

6. *Edith Wharton: A Study of Her Fiction,* Berkeley: University of California Press, 1953.

7. *Edith Wharton,* New York: Prentice Hall, 1962.

8. *Edith Wharton,* Minneapolis: University of Minnesota Press, 1964. *Edith Wharton: A Woman in Her Time,* London: Michael Joseph, 1972.

reestablished as one of the few major American novelists, and most of her works are now available in print. There have been one or two interesting specialist studies and she gets her steady quota of entries each year in the MLA bibliography. However, R. W. B. Lewis's huge biography[9] tends to crack under its own weight of detail, and Cynthia Wolff[10] allows her capacity for empathy to gorge itself a little too freely on Edith Wharton's creations. Both writers indeed use the novels to illuminate the life and character of Mrs. Wharton rather than attempt literary critical discussion.

Writing in the 1920s R. M. Lovett ended his study with the peroration that in a "world which has reverted towards barbarism . . . she remains for us among the voices whispering the last enchantments of the Victorian Age." This is emphatically not the way to read Edith Wharton, and it must be said that Lovett's book as a whole does not recommend this way. Indeed, the constant and energetic play of her irony very seldom permits the reader to rest in one response, nostalgic or otherwise. The cultural and social upheaval of the Second World War, more far-reaching than that during her lifetime, was not of a kind to send readers back to Edith Wharton in large numbers, but I think that in fact, if one had any interest in such matters at all, it did make one interested in what she had to say, as well as the way in which she said it (although some reviewers found such an interest disconcerting). The aftermath of accelerated social flux, not to say "barbarism," has continued to stimulate one's own reflections on Edith Wharton's analyses of and judgments on the social worlds that she knew—in the detached and critical spirit that she herself encourages. That was why I wrote this

---

9. *Edith Wharton*, London: Constable; New York: Harper and Row, 1975.
10. *A Feast of Words: The Triumph of Edith Wharton*, New York: Oxford University Press, 1977.

book and why I am bringing it out again.

When I planned this study I determined to confine
my attention to Edith Wharton's writings, with mere
asides on her life and personality where these seemed
relevant to literary criticism. At that time there was little
information about Mrs. Wharton as a person. *A Backward Glance,* though a splendid autobiography, is decidedly reticent. Percy Lubbock added some revealing
anecdotes and impressions. One was avid for more. Millicent Bell[11] was the first to show us not only the woman
of letters but also the woman of business, and Leon Edel
in his final volume on James[12] gave us the story of her
friendship with the master. Louis Auchincloss provided,
besides appreciation, a fascinating and very revealing
selection of photographs. This brings us to the end of
the period of restriction on the Wharton papers at Yale
in 1968, indeed just beyond it. The biographical situation has, of course, changed. Wayne Andrews[13] had
been allowed to cull some tantalizing snippets from the
diary of 1908, but now we are almost embarrassed in
both senses of the word by the revelations of R. W. B.
Lewis. However, if one keeps one's head critically, I do
not think that these biographical details affect the final
estimate of Edith Wharton as a writer. One naturally
modifies one's hunches about the connection between
certain characters and situations in the novels and the
author's own character and experience, but one still has
to try to form one's opinions of the literary quality of the
books by the exercise of one's critical sensibility.
Whether one has succeeded one's fellow critics must
decide.

I wish to express again my thanks to the library of
Yale University for allowing me to see and use what was

---

11. *Edith Wharton and Henry James,* London: Peter Owen, 1966, appendix.
12. *Henry James: The Master,* London: Hart Davis, 1972.
13. Introduction to *Best Stories of Edith Wharton,* New York: Scribner's,
1958.

then unpublished, though nonrestricted, material. I am grateful, as I acknowledge in footnotes, to a number of scholars and critics—particularly Blake Nevius and, of course, R. W. B. Lewis—for invaluable information and for quoted material not yet published in full.

Finally, I must acknowledge the debt I owe to friends with whom I have discussed Edith Wharton, her books, and her artistic interests, especially J. R. Lander, whose conversation was a considerable help long ago in the inevitably limited, though otherwise in so many ways delightful, circumstances of the University of Ghana.

Acknowledgments

I should like to thank the following publishers for permission to quote from copyrighted material:
The Oxford University Press, Inc., for permission to quote from *The Notebooks of Henry James* (1947), edited by F. O. Matthiessen and K. Murdock.
Charles Scribner's Sons, Inc., for permission to quote from the following books by Henry James: *The Portrait of a Lady* (1908) (Preface) and *Notes on Novelists* (1914).

EDITH WHARTON
A Critical Interpretation

1 The Writer and Her Work

Edith Wharton was born in 1862 into one of those New York families that antedated in their established position the famous millionaires of the turn of the century and are sometimes referred to as an aristocracy. She remarks in *A Backward Glance* that, though in youth she would have smiled at this suggestion, in the light of later events she can see its meaning, and she concludes her chapter of family history with a brilliant and penetrating summary of their habits and outlook:

My readers, by this time, may be wondering what were the particular merits, private or civic, of these amiable persons. Their lives, as one looks back, certainly seem lacking in relief; but I believe their value lay in upholding two standards of importance in any community, that of education and good manners, and of scrupulous probity in business and private affairs. New York has always been a commercial community and in my infancy the merits and defects of its citizens were those of a mercantile middle class. The first duty of such a class was to maintain a strict standard of uprightness in affairs; and the gentlemen of my father's day did maintain it, whether in the law, in banking, shipping or wholesale commercial enterprises. I well remember the horror excited by any irregularity in affairs, and the relentless social ostracism inflicted on the families of those who lapsed from professional or business integrity. In one case, where two or three men of high social standing were involved in a discreditable bank failure, their families were made to suffer to a degree that would seem merciless to our modern judgement. But perhaps the New Yorkers of that day were unconsciously trying to atone for their culpable neglect of state and national politics

17

from which they had long disdainfully held aloof, by upholding the sternest principles of business probity, and inflicting
the severest social penalties on whoever lapsed from them. At
any rate I should say that the qualities justifying the existence
of our old society were social· amenity and financial incor-
ruptibility; and we have travelled far enough from both to
begin to estimate their value.

The weakness of the social structure of my parents' day was
a blind dread of innovation, an instinctive shrinking from
responsibility. In 1824 (or thereabouts) a group of New York
gentlemen who were appointed to examine various plans for
the proposed laying-over of the city, and whose private sympathies were notoriously anti-Jeffersonian and undemocratic,
decided against reproducing the beautiful system of squares,
circles and radiating avenues which Major L'Enfant, the
brilliant French engineer, had designed for Washington, because it was thought "undemocratic" for citizens of the new
republic to own building-plots which were not all of exactly
the same shape, size and value! This naif document, shown
to me by Robert Minturn, a descendant of a member of the
original committee, and doubtless often since published,
typified the prudent attitude of a society of prosperous business
men who have no desire to row against the current. [Edith
Wharton, *A Backward Glance*, Charles Scribner's Sons, Chap.
I. Copyright 1933 Edith Wharton; renewal copyright 1961
William R. Tyler. Quoted by permission.]

The relationship of manners to morals and of both to
religious tradition is made very plain here. Yvor Winters
might well have quoted this in the chapter in *Maule's
Curse* in which he sees Edith Wharton's work as even
more closely tied than James's to the Puritan Calvinist
tradition. I think that Winters overstates his case, mainly
because he uses *The Age of Innocence* as his only example,
but the background of traditional sanctions is indeed
traceable throughout her work. One learns, however, in
the early pages of the autobiography that her family also
had an interest in field sports and horses, though not in
racing, that they made "an almost pagan" cult of good
looks in both sexes, and that they imported their women's

clothes from Paris—we learn in *The Age of Innocence* that smart men's clothes came, as one might expect, from London. They were connoisseurs of food and wine, and dining out was a principal form of entertainment. As a small child, Edith Wharton once said that her life's ambition was to be "the best-dressed woman in New York." Judged by the early photograph in *A Backward Glance,* she did pretty well in this respect and Percy Lubbock tells us several stories of her devotion to her wardrobe. The point that, at the risk of seeming frivolous, needs making is that there is surely a fairly simple connection between Mrs. Wharton's personal elegance, her taste in domestic architecture, and her literary medium. Without implying any superficial conception of style as an applied adornment, one can say that in her case it began with a more than Jamesian epigrammatic polish, developed to a dignified and undemonstrative richness of texture in her mature work, and, if it sometimes became a little dowdy late in life, never lost the air of good society. One can say of her with even more truth than E. M. Forster once said of Virginia Woolf,[1] that she always wrote as a lady. We have perhaps come far enough from the 1930s to view the fact objectively. It is difficult to see how her criticism could have been so circumstantial if she had not been a hereditary member of the upper-middle-class world; Cornelius Vanderbilt's mistaken bracketing of her with Isadora Duncan[2] as an outsider can be offset by Percy Lubbock's story of her encounter with a duchess.[3] Her criticisms are emphatically made from the inside, though her ultimate ideals have a more general human sanction; the unpleasant characters are usually in the first place vulgarians. Though she could see that the finer spirits found the sedate, unenterprising, well-to-do world claus-

---

1. *Virginia Woolf*, Cambridge: The University Press, 1942, p. 24.
2. *The Vanderbilt Feud*, London: Hutchinson, 1957, p. 170.
3. "Those dreadful women, we don't see them at home. . ." *Portrait of Edith Wharton*, London: Cape, 1947, p. 112.

trophobic, she could also see that many people failed as men and women merely by the standards of the club and the drawing-room. As she says of the manners of her childhood, "one was polite, considerate of others, careful of accepted formulas, because such were the principles of the well-bred."

Edith Wharton's family background provided her directly or indirectly with more artistic and intellectual training than perhaps she herself allows for; it was more than the standard education of a 19th-century young lady:

> I used to say that I had been taught only two things in my childhood: the modern languages and good manners. Now that I have lived to see both these branches of culture dispensed with, I perceive that there are worse systems of education. But in justice to my parents I ought to have named a third element in my training; a reverence for the English language as spoken according to the best usage. Usage, in my childhood, was as authoritative an element in speaking English as tradition was in social conduct. And it was because our little society still lived in the reflected light of a long-established culture that my parents, who were far from intellectual, who read little and studied not at all, nevertheless spoke their mother tongue with scrupulous perfection, and insisted that their children should do the same.
>
> This reverence for the best tradition of spoken English—an easy idiomatic English, neither pedantic nor "literary"—was no doubt partly due to the fact that, in the old New York families of my parents' day, the children's teachers were often English. My mother and her sisters and brother had English tutors and governesses, and my own brothers were educated at home by an extremely cultivated English tutor. In my mother's family, more than one member of the generation preceding hers had been educated at Oxford or Cambridge, and one of my own brothers went to Cambridge.
>
> Even so, however, I have never quite understood how two people so little preoccupied with letters as my father and mother had such sensitive ears for pure English. The example they set me was never forgotten; I still wince under my mother's ironic smile when I said that some visitor had stayed "quite a while," and her dry: "Where did you pick that up?"

[margin note:] EW picks up male language

The wholesome derision of my grown-up brothers saved me from pomposity as my mother's smile guarded me against slovenliness; I still tingle with the sting of their ridicule when, excusing myself for having forgotten something I had been told to do, I said, with an assumption of grown-up dignity (*aetat* ten or eleven) : "I didn't know it was imperative."

Such elementary problems as (judging from the letters I receive from unknown readers) disturb present-day users of English in America—perplexity as to the distinction between "should" and "would"—and the display of such half-educated pedantry as saying "gotten" and "you would better"—never embarrassed our speech. We spoke naturally, instinctively good English, but my parents always wanted it to be better, that is, easier, more flexible and idiomatic. This excessive respect for the language never led to priggishness, or precluded the enjoyment of racy innovations. [*A Backward Glance,* Chap. III. Quoted by permission.]

This basic linguistic culture, more assured than that of many modern linguistic scholars, was backed up by her "omniverous" reading in her family's library. The library was not large, but she found there both the older French and English classics and the standard early 19th-century writers. There were some odd gaps, and her mother exercised a rather irrational control over her novel reading, for novelists, except Scott, and their works were of dubious social status. However, she got to know the great poets and dramatists, English, French, and German, long before, as an amusing anecdote shows, she could fully understand their themes; one wonders at what age, if at all, she read the original *Custom of the Country*.[4] She read the travel books and the popular art histories of the day and she developed strong intellectual interests from reading, among others, Coleridge, Pascal, and Darwin, and also her brother's textbooks of logic and philosophy. It seems to me that, speaking generally and allowing for

---

4. By Beaumont and Fletcher. The anecdote concerns her explanation of adultery in terms of fares on the ferry boat. See *A Backward Glance,* New York: Appleton-Century, 1934, p. 73.

the limitations of life in post-Civil War upper-class New York, Edith Wharton had a superb start as a novelist. Haphazard and governess-directed though it obviously was, she had a traditional humane education. Despite restrictions and taboos, literature was part of her life from childhood onwards and she moved from one author to another as her enthusiasm urged her. She became, as Edmund Wilson says, "a tremendous blue-stocking"—decidedly in the metaphorical sense, of course. Her strong impulse to create, dating from earliest childhood though suspended till her middle thirties, saved her from the less admirable aspects of conventionality, the provincialism and the refined philistinism of the leisured society of that ugly and, she tells us, squalid city. Given her love of literature, her strength of character, and her creative power, she was able to make the most of her opportunities for self-cultivation and later to contemplate, understand, and describe ironically an isolated civilization in decline and transformation. As wife and hostess, she belonged to Society; as novelist, she analyzed its customs and attitudes for their human significance and value. Would she have been a better novelist if she had been less involved, now and later, in social life? She certainly never endorsed wholeheartedly the values of any social group, least of all her own by birth. She might perhaps have found more satisfying, and, from the point of view of some modern readers, more satisfactory, positives in another age or another place. But this is a hypothetical question and a speculative answer. More illustrious practitioners of all the arts have been more worldly than she was, in very worldly, though perhaps more cultivated, societies. But—after all—environment does not determine genius in this simple way, nor is an author's personal life necessarily the determining factor in his work.

We have long known that Edith Wharton's marriage to a wealthy Bostonian, older than herself and without occupation or interests except rather vaguely in sport and travel, was not a happy one. Leon Edel[5] tells us a good deal by the way and R. W. B. Lewis[6] naturally goes into detail; Edward Wharton's idleness seems to have led to increasing irresponsibility—including embezzlement of her trust funds—and adultery. But though he provided her with ample grounds for the divorce of 1913, she also had an affair with the remarkable and versatile philanderer, Morton Fullerton, during the years 1907–1910, which James, who was a friend of Fullerton's as well as of hers, knew all about but which was kept from everyone else, except perhaps Howard Sturgis. Her powerful Whitmanesque poem, "Terminus,"[7] emerged directly from this love affair, and one can see now that the range of her work was based on more direct personal experience and on a more passionate nature than one had fully realized previously. But her interest in life and the scope of her imagination had been very wide from the start. One comes back, as with the social themes, to what she actually wrote.

The New York books present a changing society in great detail, made significant not only socially but morally. The satire in *The House of Mirth* and *The Custom of the Country* has sources deeper than social disapproval or even indignation; there is, though the social code may be involved all the time, an underlying sense of human dignity and integrity, of pity for weakness, and of anger at malice and cruelty. Hence Lily Bart is a tragic heroine, and Undine Spragg a fiend as well as a comic adventuress. The New England tragedies spring from the same source; however paralyzing the grip of the environment on the character may appear to be, their fatalism is deeply imbedded in human sympathy and understanding. Edith

5. *Op. cit., passim.*
6. *Op. cit.*, Chapters 11, 12, 13, and 14 especially.
7. Quoted in Lewis, *op. cit.*, pp. 259–60.

Wharton's own preface to *The House of Mirth,* written
for the World Classics edition in 1936, shows how well
she understood what she was doing in portraying the per-
manently human in the modes of a particular time and
place; she in fact anticipates all Edmund Wilson's criticism
of her work.

Edith Wharton's first written effort, at the age of eleven,
which began: " 'Oh, how do you do, Mrs. Brown?' said
Mrs. Tompkins. 'If only I had known you were coming
to call I should have tidied up the drawing-room' " shows
that she was indeed almost predestined to become an
interpreter of upper-class life, while her mother's crushing
comment " 'Drawing-rooms are always tidy' " forms an
excellent indication of her need for observation and experience. She seems equally to have been predestined to
become a follower of Henry James and one early novel
is plainly derivative from his early work. When, after
achieving celebrity with her collaborative book on *The
Decoration of Houses* (with several drawing-rooms) and
establishing herself as a novelist, she eventually became a
close friend of the Master, she was, Percy Lubbock tells
us, the only woman whom he regarded as an equal and
they were "more and more never apart." It was a very
close and lively friendship; indeed, for the sedentary
James, sometimes a "reign of terror" when the
"firebird" alighted from her motor to pick him up and
carry him off on a round of country house visits.[8] The
literary relationship was equally vigorous. He was critical of her and she of him, he wishing to "tether" her "to
native pastures," she deploring the lack of local habitation for the characters in his later work.[9] Both, however,
laid great stress on organic unity and close writing in the

8. Leon Edel, *op. cit., passim.*
9. *The Letters of Henry James,* ed. P. Lubbock, London: Macmillan, 1920, 1:
404. and *A Backward Glance,* pp. 190–91.

novel. The principal idea in her early essay, "The Criticism of Fiction,"[10] that the whole development of a novel should be implicit "in germ on the first page" is expounded at length in *The Writing of Fiction* (1925). Along with the influence of James went that of her cousin by marriage, Paul Bourget, one of the first international literary figures whom she met and whom she, perhaps for this reason, always overrated. He also was a practitioner of the novel as an art, but his addiction to the "problem" novel may have been responsible for some of her less happy productions.

The all-embracing theme of Edith Wharton's earlier work is the relationship, usually a hostile relationship, between the individual and society. As has been indicated, she came of a small and in many respects obsolescent community, but its basic ideals were taken over by the more grandiose and expansive commercial dynasties that succeeded it. Social ambitions soared and moral codes loosened, but merely doing as one liked was still inconceivable. The fragment *Disintegration*, which is the beginning of a study of the effects of irresponsible wealth, containing at least one brilliant scene, seems planned to lead up to a rehabilitation of straying sheep and a refolding of the flock on more open pastures. Lionel Trilling has written on the immense importance of social class with all its connotations as giving substance to the novel. Indeed, he seems prepared almost to explain the American novel out of existence:

> In this country the real basis of the novel has never existed—that is, the tension between a middle class and an aristocracy which brings manners into observable relief as the living representation of ideals and the living comment on ideas. Our class structure has been extraordinarily fluid; our various upper classes have seldom been able or stable enough to

---

10. *Times Literary Supplement*, 14 May 1914.

establish their culture as authoritative.[11]

Edith Wharton knew an aristocrat when she saw one and
did not attempt to foist any unreal conflicts on the American scene. She does, however, present a conflict between
two distinct upper middle classes running through parts
of *The House of Mirth* and, more obviously, with foreign
noble allies on the wing, in *The Custom of the Country*.
Madame de Treymes has a foreign setting and *The Reef*
is mainly concerned with individual conflict against a
Franco-American upper-class background. In *The Fruit
of the Tree*, where part of the conflict is shifted down the
social scale and becomes a phase in the class war, the main
interest is again focused on individuals. In all these books
the individual involves himself—or herself, for Edith
Wharton was a great creator of heroines—in a prolonged
and complicated struggle with the conventions of manners
and morality, both public and private, which had been so
long established among the upper classes of Western
Europe and the eastern states of American before the First
World War that they could be taken for granted as an
unquestioned and unquestionable code of civilization.
There might be movements of groups and shifts of influence within the order, the attitude to wealth and how
it was acquired might change, ostentatious living might
be variously regarded, but Edith Wharton's mother would
have understood what Mrs. Grace Wilson Vanderbilt
meant when—rightly or wrongly—she told her son not to
refer to a working woman as a lady.[12] In her very early
historical novel, *The Valley of Decision,* Edith Wharton
had carried the theme of individual rebellion back into
Italy in the age of enlightened despotism. In the New
England novels she shows us the plight of the individual,

---

11. *The Liberal Imagination,* London: Secker, 1951, p. 260.
12. See *The Vanderbilt Feud,* p. 156.

rather than his rebellion, within the equally distinct and stable lower social strata. Everywhere she shows a deep sense of the value of mutual understanding and toleration and also of the meaning and value of forms and decencies; her friend, the historian Gaillard Lapsley, once remarked that "she was possessed of a sense of compassion deeper and more authentic than [he had] ever seen in any human being."[13]

In these earlier novels and stories she presents her chief characters against the background of a complex and changing, if still restricted, society, the whole studied with a depth of understanding that gives it the quality of a microcosm. This work has a richness and solidity that make it at least comparable to the early work of James. Physical detail and details of social custom are much more precisely and thoroughly presented than in his work, without losing their lasting and, as one says, universal appeal. The tremendous sense of the social hierarchy and of the meaning of class relationships, which one sees both in her novels and in her autobiography, reminds one not only of James but also of her other close friend and compatriot, Howard Sturgis. Sturgis was of course the complete expatriate, and one might suggest that in all three writers their fascinated and intimate participation in the upper-class life of France and Great Britain gave them a special awareness of distinctions, more conscious, because acquired, than the awareness the native writer would possess by inheritance. Possibly this in turn assisted James and Edith Wharton to see and describe the society in which they were brought up more thoroughly and objectively. Mrs. Wharton was a snob, but she had plenty to be snobbish about. It would be hard to find parallels to the picture of stupid extravagance, ostentation, and, in many cases, sheer "conspicuous waste" that one finds in Cor-

---

13. Lubbock, p. 181.

nelius Vanderbilt's memoirs or Elizabeth Drexel's *King Lehr and the Gilded Age*. Millionaire Newport contributed very little to the evolution of American architecture.[14] Edith Wharton's *Decoration of Houses* was an attempt to base a new start on the refined good taste of the French 18th century and had considerable influence. If Edith Wharton found her values mainly in the simpler but more exclusive world of Washington Square, she was, as we have seen, fully aware of its spiritual and intellectual limitations.

Mrs. Wharton spent a great part of her life from 1907 onwards in Paris, and one sees from *A Backward Glance* the extent of her acquaintance with the literary and artistic world and with Society. She was a most devoted francophile. To her, France stood for most of the traditional values of civilization as she understood it, and in 1914, when the whole fabric was in danger, this attitude inspired her practical work in building up the huge refugee organizations, the *Accueil Franco-Belge* and the *Accueil Franco-Américain*. Immediately after the war she put into book form a number of articles on what had almost been lost. *French Ways and Their Meaning* (1919) is a piece of higher *vulgarisation*, which on the whole has not outlived its original purpose, but her remark that in France the uneducated "instead of dragging the standard of culture down to their own level, and ridiculing knowledge as the affectation of a self-conscious clique . . . are obliged to esteem it, to pretend to have it, and to try to talk its language—which is not a bad way of beginning to acquire it" might be profitably considered today by anti-elitists and other enthusiasts for popular culture. The war left her exhausted both physically and emotionally. Many friends had been killed; James was dead;

---

14. See A. F. Downing and V. J. Scully, *The Architectural Heritage of Newport, Rhode Island*, Cambridge: Harvard University Press, 1952, for the entirely derivative work of the opulent period.

Sturgis died in 1920. All this naturally had a great effect on her work. It seems to be a generally accepted opinion that Edith Wharton's powers declined beyond recovery during the 1920s and that her later novels were fit for no better public than that of the women's magazines where they were serialized before publication in book form. There has been speculation as to whether or not the decline was an enforced and deliberate effort to meet the taste of a public whose purveyors paid handsomely for the prestige of her name. We now know from R. W. B. Lewis's research[15] that she was well-off to the end, but, apart from maintaining her own extremely expensive way of life, she was compelled to publish stories in periodicals below her usual level by the need to support her many dependents, especially her sister-in-law, Mary Cadwalader Jones, but also retired servants and others to whose welfare she made donations from time to time. As regards the essential literary question, one must state firmly, and nowadays it would, I think, be agreed by most critics who have given thought to the matter, that her powers as a novelist did not collapse, though one freely admits that all her later work is not of equal merit. She gives us in *A Backward Glance* an account of her artistic circumstances that seems in the main immediately acceptable, whatever objections may be raised against certain details in the book. *The Age of Innocence* was an escape into "childish memories of a long-vanished America." It is a *tour de force,* but should not be overrated to the detriment of all her later work. She finally attempted to put her war experience into serious artistic form in *A Son at the Front,* which she had brooded over for more than four years, but the result, despite certain powerful lines of irony, is heavily sentimental in outlook and crude in detailed treatment.

---

15. *Op. cit.,* Part Six, *passim.*

After it she thought of ceasing to write; she felt, very much as E. M. Forster has told us he also felt,[16] "incapable of transmuting the raw material of the after-war world into a work of art." Her attempt to do so in *The Mother's Recompense* justifies her fears. But in *Twilight Sleep* and *The Children* we find a revival of her old creative energy and narrative skill along with the play of irony, albeit of a rather less subtle kind, which is the distinguishing feature of her best work. As a writer Edith Wharton deals as surely and decisively with the world of Scott Fitzgerald as she did with him in person at the famous tea-party (or was it luncheon?) at the Pavillon Colombe.[17] The fact that she based her accounts of New York on hearsay, which, as Percy Lubbock tells us, she received with fascinated disgust, makes them the more remarkable in their vitality.

Edith Wharton's main interest as a novelist remained social. The early work, as has been indicated, records the conflicts of the individual with the conventions and customs of a still strong and organized community; *The Custom of the Country* is the comedy of a pyrrhic victory by an individual. The novels from *Twilight Sleep* onwards deal with the helplessness of individuals—the plural is appropriate here—in a Society scattered without much differentiation on both sides of the Atlantic, where conflict that can lead to tragedy is no longer possible. Edith Wharton is very critical indeed of the world in which Gatsby flourished and Dick Diver disintegrated, quite as critical as she was of the pre-1914 millionaire world, but the problem is different. Now there are neither established forms of humbug nor established forms of goodness to which the humbug can cling. In *The Writing of Fiction*

---

16. "E. M. Forster on his Life and Books," *The Listener*, 61: 1553 (1959).
17. See Arthur Mizener. *The Far Side of Paradise*, Boston: Houghton Mifflin, 1949, p. 184, and letter in the *Times Literary Supplement*, 7 July 1966.

Edith Wharton says that a novelist's work should bear "a recognizable relation to a familiar social and moral standard." The standard, as she presents it in these books, has lost its group sanctions and become a matter of individual sincerity and generosity.

Mrs. Wharton reviewed her relationship to the prose fiction of her native land and replied to her critics, contemporary and future, in a fine article, "The Great American Novel."[18] From this she went on, in *Hudson River Bracketed* and *The Gods Arrive,* to deal with the problem of the individual and society in an extreme form, namely that of the modern artist. Her last and unfinished novel, *The Buccaneers,* represents a significant new development. One senses that a vision of social reintegration would have emerged from the completed work. In fact Edith Wharton's work as a whole gives one a sense of continuous growth and inner development. A fine sensibility is responding imaginatively to changing circumstances. It is not however of the widest imaginative grasp and adaptability. It is decidedly a critical and a judging sensibility. Mrs. Wharton was also a pioneer realist who remembered that she had once been asked, " 'Have you ever known a respectable woman? If you have, in the name of decency write about her!' " and, though she satirized them severely, she did not flinch from the 1920s. She never saw much interest in "the man with the dinner-pail," as she described him. Her main achievement belongs to her "few yards of town-pavement"[19]; but, as with James, how much takes place there!

18. *The Yale Review*, 16, n.s., 1927.
19. Percy Lubbock's phrase used of James, in Preface to *The Letters*, 1: xxv.

2 Early Novels and Art and
Travel Books

Edith Wharton's first full-scale book was drafted in collaboration with a practicing architect, but in rewriting it under Walter Berry's guidance, she was, so she tells us, "taught whatever she knew about the writing of clear concise English." *The Decoration of Houses* was, in 1897, an original work on its subject, with no immediate predecessors, which was reprinted again and again and remained an inspiration to architects on both sides of the Atlantic for many years. Considered in all its aspects—its style, its erudition, its principles and precepts, its cultural and social presuppositions, and its limitations and omissions— it is a very typical expression of its author's genius and tells us of a great deal about what to expect in her creative work. *The Decoration of Houses* was written at a time when the plain brownstone houses of upper-class old New York were being replaced by the mansions of the newer and richer rich in a wide variety of medieval and Renaissance styles and Newport was acquiring its collection of French châteaux, Italian villas, and English manor-houses. Edith Wharton was well aware of the eclecticism of the 19th century and she was probably the first to draw attention to the divorce between architecture and interior design that had developed in the early years, resulting in the more and more sumptuous and overcrowded upholstery that she later describes in her novels; her

mother's drawing-rooms in New York, though rather
heavily draped in the customary way, look quite beautiful, however.[1] She notes a certain improvement in her
day, but she sees it as a return to 18th-century French
and 16th-century Italian principles. She would naturally
not have admired the more picturesque American styles
of the 70s and 80s but, on the other hand, she no doubt
found the palazzo-like clubs and mansions of McKim,
Mead, and White rather grandiose, although in *A Backward Glance* she refers respectfully to Charles McKim's
work and there is clearly a strong resemblance between
their general ideas and hers. She seems quite unaware
not only of the early work of Frank Lloyd Wright in
America and of *Art Nouveau* in Europe but also of the
Queen Anne movement of Shaw and Webb with its simple formality. One is amazed that, in a changing society,
anyone, let alone so alert an author as Edith Wharton,
could at thirty-five commit herself to the *obiter dictum:*

> Strive as we may for originality, we are hampered at every
> turn by the artistic tradition of over two thousand years.
> Does any but the most inexperienced architect really think
> that he can rid himself of such an inheritance? He may
> mutilate or misapply component parts of his design, but he
> cannot originate a whole new architectural alphabet. The
> chances are that he will not find it easy to invent one wholly
> new moulding. [Edith Wharton, *The Decoration of Houses,*
> Charles Scribner's Sons, Chap. I. Copyright 1925 Edith Whar-
> ton. Quoted by permission.]

However, bearing in mind some of the more overelabo-
rate examples of 19th-century pastiche, one may sympathize with her cautiousness. There is no doubt about
Edith Wharton's consciousness of those two thousand
years of artistic production. She combines most detailed
knowledge of it with very sensitive taste. Almost all of

---

1. See Louis Auchincloss, *Edith Wharton: A Woman in Her Time*, pp. 14–15.

her illustrations are of French and Italian houses, and her history of the evolution of the middle- and upper-class house is largely European; she clearly had a strong preference for 18th-century French furniture and fittings and indeed seems to show a certain ignorance of the English 18th-century in, for example, the matter of pelmets and curtains. The general technical knowledge displayed is, however, very considerable, and she had certainly digested and made her own what Ogden Codman presumably told her.

"Proportion," she says, "is the good breeding of architecture." This very revealing sentence sets up a standard that is both social and aesthetic. Simplicity, proportion, fitness for purpose, and ordinary straightforward comfort are her guiding principles. With these in mind she sets out her proposals for the drawing-room, boudoir, morning-room, ball-room, saloon, music-room, gallery, library, smoking-room, den, school-room, nurseries, and bedrooms. She is admirable on the need for harmony and for fitness for purpose in each individual room, on choice of color, and on avoidance of mass-produced "period" ornament. One sympathizes with her liking for open fires and fresh air and her recommendation of candles for lighting the drawing-room. There is not much point in saying that most of it belongs to the social habits of a vanished world. What is more interesting, apart from the underlying principles themselves, is the indication it gives of the nature of the society in which Edith Wharton began to write and of her own already developed social awareness. She begins by saying that she is writing for the rich, as only the rich can afford to experiment in housing and decoration and they are the initiators of changes of fashion, a remark that is in the main true but not likely to arouse popularity. Her comments on the American habit of decorating rooms for daily use in the style of European gala-rooms and of making the family drawing-room useless with uncomfortable splendor in what was really, in any case, the tradition of the "best parlour" rather than the *salon de compagnie* show that she was advising a newly rich class that had not yet found stability—the Dorsets and, even more obviously, the Wellington Brys of the novels. Nevertheless, she does not advocate a return to the dreary plainness of pre-Civil War days, but rather to the tasteful splendor of ages that were civilized as well as wealthy. *The Decoration of Houses* introduces her early work. The social conflicts and the individual rebellions and struggles of the pre-1914 novels and stories take place against a background of imitative and often vulgar magnificence. Contrast is provided by the living-rooms of cultured unmarried lawyers with their lines of old calf bindings and deep armchairs and by the faded salons of French châteaux. In fact, allowing for her personal approach, Edith Wharton's ideas did fit in with the trends in "period" domestic architecture—the revival of interest in classical Colonial buildings in America, the Georgian and Queen Anne revivals in England, and the taste for the simpler kinds of 18th-century furniture, French and English, that preceded the modern movement. Geoffrey Scott's *Architecture of Humanism* did not appear till 1914; looking back Edith Wharton describes it as "well-nigh perfect," and one can see that she had been thinking along similar lines even before they became friends. The Mount, her home at Lenox, Massachusetts, was a scaled-down version of Belton House, Grantham, Lincolnshire, England, which she had seen and specially admired, no doubt accepting the traditional, though untenable, attribution to Wren. Her own and Edward Wharton's ancestors had built similarly in the 18th century. With its white walls and broad terrace, often covered by a huge awning, the Mount belongs as much to the tradition of the New England Colonial mansion as to the British Queen Anne Revival. It does not seem that her taste changed greatly over the years. Though Henry James said: "No one fully knows our Edith who has not seen her in the act of creating a habitation for herself,"[2] homelike, let alone homely, would hardly be used as a descriptive epithet for anything she did. She remained faithful to an aesthetically unadulterated, but of course, more hygienic, French eighteenth century. The full reunification of architectural planning and interior decoration that has been a principal feature of the modern movement does not seem to have aroused her interest. Fundamentally she seems to have been one of those cultivated well-to-do women who shrink from originality in the visual arts. She surveyed society in a far more adventurous spirit, but here also, though she shocked Charles Eliot Norton,[3] she did not often depart from traditional ideals of moral and social order and her later novels seem to move toward a reconciliation of tradition with the modernity of the day. One can see that the critic both of other people's houses and of their manners and customs is the same conservative and snobbish, practical and common-sensed, discriminating and elegant Mrs. Wharton.

Edith Wharton's first novels and collections of stories were most elegant little volumes in every way. Scribners turned them out in black boards with panels of Pompeian arabesque in gold and their content belongs to the literary and artistic offshoots of the New York and Newport society in which she had spent her early married life. The style is often epigrammatic beyond that of her model, Henry James, as, for example, in "The electric lights were dissolving in the grey alembic of the dawn" or "Genius is

---

2. Lubbock, p. 129. Photographs of the interiors of the Mount and the Pavillon Colombe lend support to the supposition that follows. The Pavillon Colombe is of course a small historic showplace. Cyril Connolly's *Les Pavillons* (London: H. Hamilton, 1962) contains some beautiful photographs of its interior; restoration was begun by Mrs. Wharton and Connolly comments on the flawless taste of her work.

3. See Chapter 3 below.

of small use to a woman who does not know how to do her hair," which remind one of Wilde's preciosity. The dialogue is highly stylized, and Browning and the Rossettis and the lesser cinquecento artists often provide a conversational allusion. *The Greater Inclination*, 1899, which was a great success in both New York and London, is a carefully made selection of her stories over about eight years. It is obviously the work of a very painstaking and intelligent writer and has some unity of theme. Three stories are outstanding as having a depth of human interest and an ironical astringency in the telling that look forward to the work of her maturity. *The Muse's Tragedy* and *The Pelican* deal in different ways with the large theme of appearance and reality. In the first Mrs. Anerton, who has lived on a reputation as the Sylvia of an eminent poet, discovers late in life in company with one of his younger admirers "all that [she has] missed"; a very delicate balance is struck between pathos and absurdity by means of putting the explanation of the situation into her words. *The Pelican* combines pathos with farce. Mrs. Amyot is a caricature of the pseudo-intellectual; she is a self-established professional lecturer to small-town cultural groups and women's associations:

> Punctually at the hour appointed, we took our seats in a lecture-hall full of strenuous females in ulsters. Mrs. Amyot was evidently a favorite with these austere sisters, for every corner was crowded, and as we entered a pale usher with an educated mispronunciation was setting forth to several dejected applicants the impossibility of supplying them with seats.
>
> Our own were happily so near the front that when the curtains at the back of the platform parted, and Mrs. Amyot appeared, I was at once able to establish a comparison between the lady placidly dimpling to the applause of her public and the shrinking drawing-room orator of my earlier recollections.
>
> Mrs. Amyot was as pretty as ever, and there was the same curious discrepancy between the freshness of her aspect and

the staleness of her theme but something was gone of the blushing unsteadiness with which she had fired her first random shots at Greek art. It was not that the shots were less uncertain, but that she now had an air of assuming that, for her purpose, the bull's-eye was everywhere, so that there was no need to be flustered in taking aim. This assurance had so facilitated the flow of her eloquence that she seemed to be performing a trick analogous to that of the conjuror who pulls hundreds of yards of white paper out of his mouth. From a large assortment of stock adjectives she chose, with unerring deftness and rapidity, the one that taste and discrimination would most surely have rejected, fitting out her subject with a whole wardrobe of slop-shop epithets irrelevant in cut and size. To the invaluable knack of not disturbing the association of ideas in her audience, she added the gift of what may be called a confidential manner—so that her fluent generalizations about Goethe and his place in literature (the lecture was, of course, manufactured out of Lewes's book) had the flavor of personal experience, of views sympathetically exchanged with the audience on the best way of knitting children's socks, or of putting up preserves for the winter. It was, I am sure, to this personal accent—the moral equivalent of her dimple—that Mrs. Amyot owed her prodigious, her irrational success. It was her art of transposing second-hand ideas into first-hand emotions that so endeared her to her feminine listeners. [Edith Wharton, "The Pelican," in *The Greater Inclination,* Charles Scribner's Sons. Copyright 1927 Edith Wharton. Quoted by permission.]

Her exposure is both tragic and comic. She is neither a mere figure of fun nor a mere fraud; she is a study in sincerely convinced self-delusion, and her son in a preposterous filial piety. Edith Wharton was to return to the lecturer theme several times and in several forms; she knew it as a typical American phenomenon. *Souls Belated* is her first divorce story. The situation looks forward all the way to *The Gods Arrive* of 1932. The themes of many later works, of individual freedom and the laws of society, of honesty and hyprocrisy, of the necessity of compromise and of finding a *modus vivendi* are given a brief but very sensitive and also amusing exploration.

The Touchstone, 1900, and *Sanctuary,* 1903, which were separated by the big historical novel, *The Valley of Decision,* are first attempts to write at length about contemporary life. They are again very elegant and sophisticated in both style and subject matter, and indebted in their general method to James. They are moral fables in the manner of *The Europeans,* with the characters clearly differentiated as types, the episodes very formally arranged, and the dialogue very stylized. *The Touchstone* is a fine work on a small scale, with a real sense of inner development; it dramatizes a moral problem, the lamentable discrepancy—owing to the need to keep up a social position financially—between the ideal and the actual in the married life of a New York Society couple with literary connections. The husband, Glennard, commits secretly a breach of trust and chivalry and the quality of his offence against the code of the gentleman is defined negatively by the description of his accomplice:

> Perhaps the shortest way of defining Flamel is to say that his well-known leniency of view was vaguely divined to include himself. Simple minds may have resented the discovery that his opinions were based on his perceptions; but there was certainly no more definite charge against him than that implied in the doubt as to how he would behave in an emergency, and his company was looked upon as one of those mildly unwholesome dissipations to which the prudent may occasionally yield. It now offered itself to Glennard as an easy escape from the obsession of moral problems, which somehow could no more be worn in Flamel's presence than a surplice in the street. [Edith Wharton, *The Touchstone,* Charles Scribner's Sons. Copyright 1927 Edith Wharton. Quoted by permission.]

The deterioration of his position is indicated as he overhears such remarks from his wife as "It is like listening at a keyhole. I wish I hadn't read it," while they desperately keep up appearances according to the elaborate conventions of the time. The reestablishment of confidence between them is done very subtly but with great economy. There is a slight element of sentimentality in the imagery used, the husband being like a child taking refuge against its mother's breast, the couple being like the Christians purifying pagan temples, and the ending is something of a sleight of hand:

> "Don't you see that you've never before been what she thought you, and that now, so wonderfully, she's made you into the man she loved? That's worth suffering for, worth dying for, to a woman—that's the gift she would have wished to give!"
> "Ah," he cried, "but woe to him by whom it cometh. What did I ever give her?"
> "The happiness of giving," she said. [*The Touchstone.* Quoted by permission.]

But we have been prepared for it; Glennard has been made to develop through penance and repentance into a wiser and nobler man and his wife has become a mature and sympathetic woman. *The Touchstone* keeps within the austerely elegant code of old New York. It shows that a satisfying relationship can exist and that emotional tensions can be eased within strict limits. The upper-class ideal of conduct is shown as humane and compassionate, as hostile only to deceit and cowardice. Edith Wharton tells us that the book had little success in America at the time. Today its interest is partly that of a period piece, partly that of a demonstration of the value of the social scheme, which she was later to examine so searchingly.

Van Wyck Brooks, who had no great admiration for the work of Mrs. Wharton, calls *The Valley of Decision*, 1902, a triumph of American letters.[4] As did her contemporaries, he admires the immense culture displayed, the easy and familiar acquaintance with Italian history and art—of a period, what is more, that was not usually much studied

---

4. *The Confident Years*, Chapter 16.

or esteemed. Edith Wharton herself describes it more critically as "not a novel at all, but only a romantic chronicle." She is being over modest. One may compare the book favorably with *Romola;* it also suffers from a stilted artificiality of style. *The Valley of Decision* takes place in late 18th-century Italy. There is a vast amount of historical detail derived from Edith Wharton's extensive reading, though some of it seems a little conventional—there are rather a lot of ballad-singers and mountebanks in the town scenes. She obviously enjoyed building up the visual background, which is often vivid and picturesque, and shows her thorough and precise knowledge of art and architecture as well as social customs. Running through it all is the theme of the impact of the Enlightenment and the French Revolution, and it is in fact a first full-scale treatment of the theme of rebellion against traditional forms and the conflict of the exceptional individual with the varied forces of the community. This gives the book what living interest it still has, as distinct from the fascination of its background descriptions.

The novel opens with a rich and varied presentation of the old régime, first in poverty-stricken and ostentatious Pianura, the imaginary Duchy, with a decadent Duke and a flamboyant hunting Duchess, next in efficient, priest-ridden, and snobbish Turin, and finally in a feudal castle that bears a certain resemblance to Nievo's Fratta. Out of this emerges Odo Valsecca, heir to the Duchy. He gradually comes under the influence of the ideas that produced the French Revolution and this is reinforced by his falling in love with the brilliant daughter of a liberal professor. The scene is broadened by a tour of Italy, taking in Naples with its *cognoscenti* and Venice with its empty social and political shows. This is all very skillfully done and there are many good minor characters. Odo, as the intellectual young prince, is a genuinely interesting study, and his career as Duke is made a typically 18th-century compromise. He marries the widowed Duchess for her money and keeps the dottoressa as a mistress. He sets about rapid reform and alienates all parties, from extreme clerical to extreme radical. The catastrophe comes when Fulvia, his mistress, is murdered by the mob as a witch. Odo reacts into extreme conservatism and is finally overthrown by the revolutionary movement which he has himself long been associated with. Edith Wharton probably merely tried to do her best in what she accepted as a standard literary mode. As a result the book has something of the peculiar contrived and wooden quality of so many older historical novels. There is little depth of realization anywhere or of emotional pressure to carry us forward, and one wonders how it could ever have seemed really alive to anyone. The comparison has been suggested between old New York and old Pianura. It can be made in certain respects, though old Pianura is more cultivated and more tolerant of human frailty. The Duchy, however, is a not inadequate symbol of an old order. Rebellion in the name of Rousseau and liberalism may seem also rather faded to economically and sociologically minded readers, but it meant much to Edith Wharton's generation, when the liberal individualist attitude was still an unopposed force in American public life and the Risorgimento was a living memory; she wrote one or two stories based on this theme. The old régime, the position of the church, the characters and motives of the liberals, and the behavior of the populace are presented with some sense of complexity. Odo's rebellious idealism and subsequent disillusion are very plausible, but despite the fact that Edith Wharton tells us that "about this time [he] was more real to [her] than most of the people [she] walked and talked with in [her] daily life," he fails fully to come alive on the page today. One does not ask for a mere crude hindsight in the treatment and interpretation of events, but one wishes that she had succeeded in projecting more of the feelings of her own times into the situations of the past. This would have given the novel a living interest for us today, but the idiom she uses, lacking any exact correspondence of word to feeling, limits such a personal realization of the themes as much as it inhibits energy in the narrative as narrative. It would be unfair to compare *The Valley of Decision* with Nievo's panoramic interpretation of the Revolution and its aftermath in Italy, but there is some point and justice in suggesting that Lampedusa's *The Leopard* would seem, even in translation, to make a limited piece of 19th-century history come alive as an example of social growth and change in a way that Edith Wharton's book unfortunately fails to do. She was not quite ready to tackle the social issues of her time except in short stories.

It is appropriate to pass straight from *The Valley of Decision* to Edith Wharton's two studies of Italian art and history, *Italian Villas and their Gardens*, 1904, and *Italian Backgrounds*, 1905. The first, which arose out of a commission to write a series of articles to be attached to charming but rather glamorized illustrations by Maxfield Parrish in the *Century Magazine,* has all the appearance of a lavish ladylike production in the taste of the time, but, despite a certain gush in the style, it is in fact a work of considerable amateur scholarship with only one immediate predecessor, a German study of W. C. Tuckermann published in 1884. Mrs. Wharton tells us in *A Backward Glance* a good deal about the adventurous "field work" that preceded the writing, about her refusal to be anecdotal, and her attempt, unfortunately unsuccessful, to include plans of gardens in the final volume. One must not be put off by a heading such as *Italian Garden Magic;* the chapter is an excellent exposition of general principles, as, for example, when she says of the Italian garden architect's three main problems:

. . . his garden must be adapted to the architectural lines of the house it adjoined; it must be adapted to the requirements of the inmates of the house, in the sense of providing shady walks, sunny bowling-greens, parterres and orchards, all conveniently accessible; and lastly it must be adapted to the landscape around it. At no time and in no country has this triple problem been so successfully dealt with as in the treatment of the Italian country house from the beginning of the sixteenth to the end of the eighteenth century; and in the blending of different elements, the subtle transition from the fixed and formal lines of art to the shifting and irregular lines of nature, and lastly in the essential convenience and livableness of the garden, lies the fundamental secret of the old garden-magic.

However much other factors may contribute to the total impression of charm, yet by eliminating them one after another, by *thinking away* the flowers, the sunlight, the rich tinting of time, one finds that, underlying all these, there is the deeper harmony of design which is independent of any adventitious effects. This does not imply that a plan of an Italian garden is as beautiful as the garden itself. The more permanent materials of which the latter is made—the stonework, the evergreen foliage, the effects of rushing or motionless water, above all the lines of the natural scenery—all form a part of the artist's design. But these things are as beautiful at one season as at another; and even these are but the accessories of the fundamental plan. The inherent beauty of the garden lies in the grouping of its parts—in the converging lines of its long ilex-walks, the alternation of sunny open spaces with cool woodland shade, the proportion between terrace and bowling-green, or between the height of a wall and the width of a path. None of these details was negligible to the landscape architect of the Renaissance: he considered the distribution of shade and sunlight, of straight lines of masonry and rippled lines of foliage, as carefully as he weighed the relation of his whole composition to the scene about it.

Then, again, any one who studies the old Italian gardens will be struck with the way in which the architect broadened and simplified his plan if it faced a grandiose landscape. Intricacy of detail, complicated groupings of terraces, fountains, labyrinths and porticoes, are found in sites where there is no great sweep of landscape attuning the eye to larger impressions. The farther north one goes, the less grand the landscape becomes and the more elaborate the garden. The great pleasure-grounds overlooking the Roman Campagna are laid out on severe and majestic lines: the parts are few; the total effect is one of breadth and simplicity. [Edith Wharton, *Italian Villas and Their Gardens,* Century. Copyright 1904 Edith Wharton. Quoted by permission.]

This sets the pattern for her detailed descriptions of the villas of Florence, Siena, Rome, Genoa, Lombardy, and the Veneto. She argues very cogently that the *jardin anglais,* far from being a naturalistic landscape garden, is in Italian conditions entirely exotic and artificial, especially as lawns do not grow properly in southern Europe, and she shows that all over Italy a different kind of integration of garden into orchards and vineyards was achieved, which has often been spoiled or ignored by later generations. She does not in fact say much about the houses, but concentrates her attention on the gardens. She is particularly illuminating on a garden such as Gamberaia and on the smaller and more rural Sienese villas. The great Roman villas are described very learnedly, with much valuable information. She strongly admired Lante, which she describes in great detail, and the monumental Baroque Caprarola. She would no doubt have approved the recent careful restoration of Lante to its original state with colored gravel in the beds of the parterre. The Frascati villas are compared with great discrimination. The splendidly towering Aldobrandini she finds rather immature Baroque and its magnificent water-theater out of proportion. She prefers the Lancellotti and the Falconieri. She comes out strongly as an admirer of Isola Bella, praising the stucco- and shell-lined grottoes in the palace and the whole great pyramidal garden, preserved with its original planting, which she sees as a piece of supreme fantasy in a fantastically beautiful landscape. Again Edith Wharton would surely have been delighted at the restoration of the garden in the fifties and at the completion of the palace after three centuries with a Baroque white, blue, and gold octagonal *salone* in the center of its main facade, which might have provided a further illustration of how to decorate a house on the grand scale. There are many accounts of villas, such as the 16th-century Cicogna near Varese and the Castello di Cattajo, a belated Gothic fantasy near Padua, which Edith Wharton may be said to have "discovered," and she draws attention to the Prato della Valle at Padua as a model public garden. Altogether, with its notes on architects, the book is an impressive work.

Edith Wharton's attitude to the Baroque is its most interesting general aspect. She was writing at a time when, as she says, it was little appreciated in England or America or even France. The influences of Ruskin and Viollet-le-Duc were still strong. Edith Wharton knew the German scholarly and critical works. She could have read *Renaissance and Baroque,* originally published in German in 1888, though she does not mention Wölfflin at any time. She quotes Gurlitt frequently and she is, moreover, able to point out that he does not go beyond the main outlines and overrates the influence of Palladio on later Venetian houses. In all this she was well in advance of contemporary taste and interests, though she is a little uncertain at times about her liking for certain baroque villas, unless carried away by sheer splendor, as with Isola Bella. In *Italian Backgrounds,* 1905, however, she writes at length on her admiration of the great Baroque masters Bernini, Borromini, Maderna, Guercino, the Caracci, Longhena, and, above all, Tiepolo, though still saying that theirs is an art of decadence, and asks very pertinently what would be left of Rome or Venice without their work; she calls up an amusing picture of the devoted "guide-book" tourist of the 19th century trying to see nothing except the Forum, Santa Sabina, and Santa Maria sopra Minerva. Her enthusiasm runs on into the settecento Venice and the era of her novel.

Italian Backgrounds contains a number of charming and original essays. We move down from Switzerland, "the old maid's paradise," to Brescia and its surroundings, where she describes a terracotta Stations of the Cross of remarkable artistic quality in a country church—we are told of other similar works at the Baroque sanctuaries of the Pennine Alps. The account of a visit to San Vivaldo, a remote convent near San Gimignano, contains what was a real contribution to art history; she was convinced that the terracotta statuary belonged to the della Robbia school rather than to the 17th century, as was officially stated, and she later succeeded in convincing the Director of Museums for Tuscany of this attribution. The book is full of sensitive first-hand descriptive appreciations of particular monuments. There is, for instance, an interesting chapter on Parma and Corregio and the Farnese Theatre and a fine appreciation of the monuments of Milan, ranging from the Romanesque churches to the Ospedale Maggiore and the Portinari chapel of Sant'Eustorgio.

Edith Wharton classed herself with the cultured amateurs of the previous generation, Pater, Symonds, and Vernon Lee, who had guided her own earlier travels and of whom the last was a personal friend, and she maintained that there was a place for books by such authors alongside the work of Berenson, also for many years a personal friend, and the scholars. Her later *A Motor-Flight through France*, 1908, is a fine old-fashioned travel book. It combines general observations on what was becoming her adopted country with detailed descriptions of monuments, which are in fact admirable amateur art criticism, based on a catholic and discriminating taste. It was written for her generation of cultivated New Yorkers and similar tourists. *In Morocco* is an account of a holiday in 1917, arranged for Mrs. Wharton—it is worth noting, as an indication of the level on which she liked to do things—by the Resident-General, General, later Marshal, Lyautey. It gives a fascinating picture of the mosques, the palaces, and the traditional upper-class life of another civilization before its trans-formation—a gorgeous scene of rich merchants, noble-men, and Negro slaves. With its outline of history, its note on architecture, and its bibliography, the book is a model travelogue of a short visit. Taste in travel books has shifted a long way from an interest in the visually picturesque and the melodramatically historical to sociological and gastronomic enthusiasms, but Edith Wharton's have a freshness and breadth of outlook that make them deserve reprinting where most of the other late 19th- and early 20th-century works do not. One can see from these books that the obscurer artistic allusions of her earlier novels are no mere affectation.

3 Tragedy in Society

I

There should not be any need today to apologize for the fact that Edith Wharton's great tragic novel, *The House of Mirth,* 1905, is placed in the world of the Four Hundred in the Gilded Age. Edith Wharton herself, writing in the 1930s,[1] deals admirably with contemporary and later comments on its social theme. She was a pioneer in choosing to write about New York Society, and she herself doubted, as her critics have done since, whether the material "in all its flatness and futility," was worthwhile, but in fact she triumphantly succeeds in giving her gang of "irresponsible pleasure-seekers . . . dramatic significance through what its frivolity destroys," the only significance she believed to be possible. Naturally Society was furious at the satire on its carefully guarded existence and scandalized at the sympathy with which its typical victim, the heroine, is treated. *The House of Mirth* is firmly based in its period, but I do not wish to speculate on how far the Van Osburgh "crushes" may resemble Mrs. Astor's receptions or chase any other literary-historical hares.

Edith Wharton's "simple and fairly moving domestic tragedy," as she calls it, has claims to a high place among tragic novels. If it does not belong with, say, *Wuthering Heights* or *Anna Karenina,* one can fairly place it with the tragic work of George Eliot and Henry James. It also is

1. See preface to World's Classics edition of 1936 and *A Backward Glance,*
   pp. 205–8.

49

tragedy with a particular and fully developed social setting. The broad theme is the conflict between the individual and the community. It is not so much a rebellion
against conventions as a struggle for existence. In this case
the individual struggles for position and indeed livelihood
of the kind she thinks is her due, but the community,
Society with a capital "S," is highly organized and very
strong, and in the end, however brave the individual
shows herself to be, she falls a victim to forces which no
individual could cope with alone. Edith Wharton faced
and mastered the problem of the tragic heroine in a
novel of modern social life. Henry James had worked on
this problem carefully, having in mind his predecessors,
and she learned from all of them. George Eliot, while very
aware of the fragility of the "frail vessel," gives her in the
later novels both intelligence and a developing self-awareness as well as the depth of feeling that has so often been
expatiated on. She nevertheless supports the interest of
the heroines with many subsidiary themes and centers of
consciousness. When James, looking back on his creation
of Isabel Archer, examines the problem in the Preface to
The Portrait of a Lady, and makes his famous pronouncement:

> "Place the centre of the subject in the young woman's own
> consciousness," I said to myself, "and you get an interesting
> and as beautiful a difficulty as you could wish. Stick to that—
> for the centre; put the heaviest weight into the scale, which
> will be so largely the scale of her relation to herself. Make
> her only interested enough, at the same time, in the things
> that are not herself, and this relation needn't fear to be too
> limited. Place meanwhile in the other scale the lighter weight
> (which is usually the one that tips the balance of interest) :
> press least hard, in short, on the consciousness of your heroine's
> satellites, especially the male; make it an interest contributive
> only to the greater one . . ."

one sees a clear statement of the method used by Edith

Wharton. Edith Wharton, however, attempts a rather different sequence of events. Her Lily Bart is not, like Isabel Archer, free to choose. She begins with an all-embracing inherited financial problem and with very ordinary false gods. In this sense she is nearer to George Eliot's Gwendolen Harleth, who also has tremendous charm and dignity, sensitiveness and intelligence, combined with lamentable self-ignorance. Lily Bart is not portrayed as even an aspiring intellectual, as is Isabel Archer, but she is more perceptive from the beginning as to her own character and situation, and by the end she may be said to achieve the tragic vision of her creator. One may sum up by saying that, having learned from James's example before his precept was actually formulated, Edith Wharton places the "centre of the subject [decidedly] in the young women's own consciousness" and presses "least hard . . . on the consciousness of [the] heroine's satellites, especially the male," and that from this pattern she evolves the story of Lily Bart and Lawrence Selden, which for its substance would seem also to owe a debt to George Eliot.

The close writing and dramatic planning of the novel are fundamental qualities; Edith Wharton achieves some remarkable juxtapositions of scenes and persons, and the last page, as she puts it, is indeed latent in the first. The tragic effect is cumulative. The first fifteen pages put before us Lily Bart and her predicament in the society around her. She is characteristically on the move from one house party to another at the end of the New York summer, and she commits the terrible indiscretion of returning to the flat of a young male friend, Lawrence Selden, to have tea with him. Her surrender to this temptation is described with the most delicate irony and the magnitude of the indiscretion is very quickly made plain in succeeding episodes. Lily Bart is represented as outstandingly beautiful, though slightly faded after eleven years of Society's exacting routine, and her gay conversation is made wonderfully revealing. She is "horribly poor—and very expensive" and she has lost chances of marriage because she has frightened young men's mothers by her fast habits; she smokes, for example—on this occasion she also fills up her cigarette case! Selden, however, has already seen and reflected on her inner nature behind this frivolous and even predatory exterior. For him

> Everything about her was at once vigorous and exquisite, at once strong and fine. He had a confused sense that she must have cost a great deal to make, that a great many dull and ugly people must, in some mysterious way, have been sacrificed to produce her. He was aware that the qualities distinguishing her from the herd of her sex were chiefly external: as though a fine glaze of beauty and fastidiousness had been applied to vulgar clay. Yet the analogy left him unsatisfied, for a coarse texture will not take a high finish; and was it not possible that the material was fine, but that circumstance had fashioned it into a futile shape? [Edith Wharton, *The House of Mirth*, Charles Scribner's Sons, Bk. I, 1. Copyright 1905 Edith Wharton; renewal copyright 1933 William R. Tyler. Quoted by permission.]

This impression, introduced with superbly skillful casualness, gives us a great deal of Lily Bart. The ironic implications of the analogy bring out just how subtly balanced her qualities are; Edith Wharton has calculated every phrase, for we see as the book progresses that in all her relationships Lily Bart is like this, and that everyone forms the same impression. The last question can be looked back on as a clue to her future and tragic development. However artificial her elegance may seem, it is the outward sign of a real dignity and grace of character that command admiration and respect. She is indeed a lady in a world where, despite incidental coarsening of the code, the word still had meaning; Society still explicitly subscribed to the ideal, though in practice it had often become the merest matter of outward good form. Lily

Bart has certain ideals of a civilized and cultivated life, though they have been corrupted by a corrupt Society into something parasitic and materialistic. Her tragedy results from her pursuit of these falsified ideals in the face of an increasingly hostile Society. It is a further irony that Society, as we see it, has no right to be hostile or censorious, and a further irony still that Lily Bart's good qualities are quite as fatal to her as those of which we may disapprove. The poignancy of her tragedy lies there. She is too good for Society, as Selden later feels, and consequently, though she cannot escape, she cannot play its game to the logical conclusion. Selden, who understands and foresees so much, is a type of young man who appears several times in Edith Wharton. He represents old New York, which does not otherwise contribute very much to the wealthier and newer social pattern of the novel, except insofar as the established families pay lip-service to its social forms. He is cultivated and full of good intentions, but, because of a certain excessive fastidiousness, he is sometimes ineffectual to the point of unkindness. One gathers that there were many such men in old New York Society, where the possession of adequate means or an assured professional position, as in Selden's case, combined with a retiring gentlemanly ideal, made any sort of enterprise—economic, intellectual or moral—seem unnecessary and even rather improper. Edith Wharton shows both the merits and weaknesses of the type; the heavy-handed condemnation of Selden by Edmund Wilson, for example, misses the point. Lily Bart makes a mistake of another kind when she snubs the young Jewish financier. This is an indiscretion of her fastidious good taste rather than recklessness, but the two reinforce each other and Lily is fated to be involved with Rosedale for the rest of the book. If Selden with his advice is a kind of ineffectual good angel, her association with Rosedale brings her eventually to her lowest point of degradation. At the same

time there is an implied comparison between her career
and his; she has a long start of him, but he succeeds where
she ultimately fails—because she has scruples where he
has none. Rosedale is a specially brilliant character study.

   Lily Bart is now ready to be shown to us in full career.
There is a short, gracefully comic interlude with a shy
young millionaire, the source of whose wealth is an invention of his father's for keeping fresh air out of hotels—one
of those small satiric touches that symbolize the whole social fabric. Then the first big scene opens at Bellomont,
the country house of the Trenor family, with its park, its
church near the gates, and all its domestic detail indis-
tinguishable from contemporary England, but made
slightly absurd, as with the Sunday church-going. The central Society group is created and exposed with devastating
brilliance from Mrs. Trenor, the hostess, whose

> rosy blondness had survived some forty years of futile activity
> without showing much trace of ill-usage except in a dimin-
> ished play of feature. It was difficult to define her beyond
> saying that she seemed to exist only as a hostess, not so much
> from any exaggerated instinct of hospitality as because she
> could not sustain life except in a crowd. [*The House of Mirth*,
> Bk. I, 4. Quoted by permission.]

to Mrs. Fisher, the divorcée, "her eyes and gowns as em-
phatic as her 'case,'" Lady Cressida Raith with her "eth-
nographical trinkets," and Miss Van Osburgh, "a large
girl with flat surfaces and no high lights." Again Edith
Wharton shows her genius for significant external details;
one is just sufficiently conscious of the idea of the "scarlet
woman" when Mrs. Trenor advices Lily not to wear red
at dinner. The precariousness of Lily's position comes out
painfully in the fact that, besides doing small secretarial
duties for her hostess, she has to play cards, which she
cannot afford to do, in order to fit into the pattern. She
is thus driven to hazarding the very position she is cling-

ing to. At this point we are appropriately given Lily's background, an account of her childhood in a hectic New York setting, and her youth with a mother who persistently lived beyond a not inconsiderable legacy, which together have provided her with an absolutely artificial conception of life. She can only react against her aunt, Mrs. Peniston, who represents moral atrophy in general rather than the stability of old New York; she is almost a caricature figure.

The complexity of Lily Bart becomes clearer than ever during this house-party when we see how intelligent she can be about herself and her limitations:

> She was beginning to have fits of angry rebellion against fate, when she longed to drop out of the race and make an independent life for herself. But what manner of life would it be? She had barely enough money to pay her dress-makers' bills and her gambling debts; and none of the desultory interests which she dignified with the name of tastes was pronounced enough to enable her to live contentedly in obscurity. Ah, no—she was too intelligent not to be honest with herself. She knew that she hated dinginess as much as her mother had hated it, and to her last breath she meant to fight against it, dragging herself up again and again above its flood till she gained the bright pinnacles of success which presented such a slippery surface to her clutch. [*The House of Mirth*, Bk.I, 3. Quoted by permission.]

And yet she can shortly afterwards relapse into mere passive acceptance of the world around her:

> In the rosy glow it diffused her companions seemed full of amiable qualities. She liked their elegance, their lightness, their lack of emphasis: even the self-assurance which at times was so like obtuseness now seemed the natural sign of social ascendancy. They were lords of the only world she cared for, and they were ready to admit her to their ranks and let her lord it with them. Already she felt within her a stealing allegiance to their standards, an acceptance of their limitations. a disbelief in the things they did not believe in, a contemptuous pity for the people who were not able to live as they lived. [*The House of Mirth*, Bk. I, 4. Quoted by permission.]

This vacillation is another of the sources of her tragedy.
Selden brings out all her best qualities during a magnificent scene in which a rather conventionally beautiful
landscape and romantic atmosphere are used as a background for the juxtaposition of two opposed outlooks on
life, with all the subtle implications deriving from the
two characters; Edith Wharton is ironically sympathetic
towards Lily and also shows on this occasion the full distinction of Selden. He talks of intellectual ideals opposed
to those of society and tries hard, though a little arrogantly,
to wean Lily away from her materialism. Though she is
obviously deeply moved, she prevents a serious proposal
of marriage by a trick of badinage and so maintains her
own freedom—such as we know it is. "It's you who are the
coward," he says. To him she is, but she has escaped the
poverty she knows she cannot face and she has incidentally
avoided making him unhappy; she will not make use of
him as she would of others. Alliance with Selden might
have made it possible for them to start an independent life
together, but she is already too involved with Society for
cultivated and impecunious rebellion to attract her. It is
the first real tragic turning point. The best and worst of
Lily have been roused, and they are complementary to
each other. The irony of the situation is that her very self-
respect is partly responsible for her rejection of Selden;
in any case one cannot be sure that he would have proposed spontaneously, and her association with Selden indirectly loses her the millionaire.

Her next blunder is a piece of sheer stupidity. In her
desperate financial straits she accepts an offer from Gus
Trenor to "make money" for her on the Stock Exchange.
The circumstances of this are in fact not entirely plausible
and Edith Wharton should have given more care to such
an important episode. However, the consequences fit into
the pattern and begin to appear when, after a brief,
tragically ironic encounter with Selden—it is "her fate

to appear at her worst" to him, yet he feels "in a world apart with her,"—fate indeed, in the persons of Trenor and Rosedale, bears down on her. Within the smart social setting they are made to stand for something like brute force and low cunning in alliance. Gus Trenor's appetites are made plain on every occasion; "Did you ever watch Trenor eat?" the dyspeptic George Dorset remarks in horror.

At this point, a typical recurrent phenomenon of the time manifests itself in a way that demonstrates both the fluidity of Society as a whole and the strength of the central core, while at the same time providing an appropriate background for an important scene. A new family arises to the surface, aided by Mrs. Fisher, the divorced hanger-on of Society who has twice Lily's skill but none of Lily's delicacy. She is a foil balanced at the opposite pole against Gerty Farish, the welfare worker among the poor. The Wellington Bry's first big party, of which the chief feature is a series of *tableaux vivants* based on famous pictures, is significant in several ways. *Tableaux* were a very popular form of ostentatious entertainment at the time; they had a fairly obvious sociological and psychological value in a Society without ancestry. Trenor calls it all "damned bad taste," but the reader finds considerable difficulty in differentiating between the vulgarity of old and new wealth. Lily Bart appears as a Reynolds portrait and scores a triumph:

> No other *tableau* had been received with that precise note of approval: it had obviously been called forth by herself, and not by the picture she impersonated. She had feared at the last moment that she was risking too much in dispensing with the advantages of a more sumptuous setting, and the completeness of her triumph gave her an intoxicating sense of recovered power. Not caring to diminish the impression she had produced, she held herself aloof from the audience till the movement of dispersal before supper, and thus had a second opportunity of showing herself to advantage, as the throng

poured slowly into the empty drawing-room where she was
standing. [*The House of Mirth*, Bk. I, 12. Quoted by permission.]

It is in fact the very eve of her downfall, and one sees in
her behavior, "deuced bold," by the standards of the time,
a vividly symbolic example of the indiscretion that has
been hinted at previously and that is constantly ruining
her chances of finding the wealthy security she desires. The
tragic irony of the occasion is doubled by a brief scene in
the Bry's conservatory, a sort of artificial counterpoise to
the scene in Bellomont Park; Selden, who has been dazzled
by her beauty, is once more rebuffed by the enigmatic
"Ah, love me, love me—but don't tell me so!" There is a
mixture of vanity and coquettishness with, as has already
been noted, genuine regard in her attitude to Selden; we
realize this as she meditates next morning:

> Did he really mean to ask her to marry him? She had once
> shown him the impossibility of such a hope, and his subse-
> quent behaviour seemed to prove that he had accepted the
> situation with a reasonableness somewhat mortifying to her
> vanity. It was all the more agreeable to find that this reason-
> ableness was maintained only at the cost of not seeing her;
> but, though nothing in life was as sweet as the sense of her
> power over him, she saw the danger of allowing the episode of
> the previous night to have a sequel. Since she could not marry
> him, it would be kinder to him, as well as easier for herself,
> to write a line amicably evading his request to see her: he was
> not the man to mistake such a hint, and when next they met
> it would be on their usual friendly footing.
>
> Lily sprang out of bed, and went straight to her desk. She
> wanted to write at once, while she could trust to the strength
> of her resolve. She was still languid from her brief sleep and
> the exhilaration of the evening, and the sight of Selden's
> writing brought back the culminating moment of her tri-
> umph: the moment when she had read in his eyes that no
> philosophy was proof against her power. It would be pleasant
> to have that sensation again . . . no one else could give it to
> her in its fulness; and she could not bear to mar her mood of

luxurious retrospection by an act of definite refusal. She took up her pen and wrote hastily: *"To-morrow at four";* murmuring to herself, as she slipped the sheet into its envelope: "I can easily put him off when to-morrow comes." [*The House of Mirth,* Bk. I, 13. Quoted by permission.]

She is, as it were, poised above opposing impulses when she is tricked into a visit to the Trenor mansion in the evening and finds Gus Trenor alone. She now pays the price of her indiscretions, in appearance if not in act; she defeats Trenor by a spontaneous display of all the dignity of her nature, and the social conventions assist her escape, but she feels that she is ruined; some one saw her from across the street, and in the Society of that day even such a show of ruin was as fatal as any real moral lapse. Avenging forces are already haunting her:

> She had once picked up, in a house where she was staying, a translation of the *Eumenides,* and her imagination had been seized by the high terror of the scene where Orestes, in the cave of the oracle, finds his implacable huntresses asleep, and snatches an hour's repose. Yes, the Furies might sometimes sleep, but they were there, always in the dark corners, and now they were awake and the iron clang of their wings was in her brain. [*The House of Mirth,* Bk. I, 13. Quoted by permission.]

Edith Wharton's introduction of the Eumenides, a theme which deeply impressed her also, is remarkably effective. The vision has been prepared for by many fatal circumstances and traits of character, so that when it appears it stands, without any air of melodrama or pedantry, for the power of conventions as powerful as tribal taboos. Lily takes refuge with Gerty Farish, the one character who lives an independent life yet is accepted by Society. The scene of hysteria that follows is most powerful; the Furies are now part of Lily's consciousness:

"You'll let me stay? I shan't mind when daylight comes—

Is it late? Is the night nearly over? It must be awful to be
sleepless—everything stands by the bed and stares—" [*The
House of Mirth*, Bk. I, 14. Quoted by permission.]

One feels that there is far more reality in them in this
luxurious and brutal New York world than among the
faded museum pieces of *The Family Reunion*. The reader
knows that, on the fatal occasion, it was Selden at the other
side of Fifth Avenue, in company with her uncle, Ned
Van Alstyne, who represented that chivalry which was
among the better qualities of old New York. The reader
also knows that Selden had, before that episode, thoroughly analyzed his feelings for Lily and decided that,
with full knowledge of both Lily and himself, he was in
love with her. If Selden had stood completely apart from
the Society he lived in, he might have preserved his belief
in Lily, but that would have needed a different book.
Selden fails Lily at this point, though with very good reasons by the code of the time. Lily has failed him too; we
know her hesitations have been only partly disinterested
and that she had intended to refuse him up to the previous fateful day. However, she is again alone in the world
and nearer still to the end of her resources, partly because
of her indiscretion and frivolity and partly because of her
dignity, moral honesty, and sincerity. Lily Bart rises to
the occasion once again. As she has preserved her chastity
from Trenor, she preserves her integrity of character from
Rosedale—although less conclusively. In a scene of con-
summately presented vulgarity he offers marriage as a
sound deal:

> "Oh, if you mean you're not dead in love with me, I've got
> sense enough left to see that. And I ain't taking to you as if
> you were—I presume I know the kind of talk that's expected
> under those circumstances. I'm confoundedly gone on you—
> that's about the size of it—and I'm just giving you a plain
> business statement of the consequences. You're not very fond
> of me yet—but you're fond of luxury, and style, and amuse-

ment, and of not having to worry about cash. You like to
have a good time, and not to have to settle for it; and what I
propose to do is to provide for the good time and do the set-
tling." [*The House of Mirth*, Bk. I, 15. Quoted by permission.]

She manages to delay a decision, and it is the measure of
her present plight that we are left in doubt as to whether
she would have accepted Rosedale or not. A temporary,
and almost symbolic, escape now offers itself in the shape
of an invitation to cruise in the Mediterranean, and from
now on the reader watches her position become progres-
sively more precarious.

Book II opens in April in the Monte Carlo of the Grand
Dukes, and an even more nomadic life begins for Lily
Bart. The Furies are in pursuit and, as Edith Wharton
records of the writing, "the tale rushes onwards towards
its climax"; the technique is a crescendo of comparable
episodes. The life of the Riviera makes one look forward
twenty years to Scott Fitzgerald, but of course, though hectic, it is far more magnificent and highly organized than in
the 20s and every adventure is also a far more serious
breach of decorum. There is rather more scope for indiscretion than in the closely confined New York setting, but
the theme of contrasted manners is not developed in this
instance. To Selden, who is also on holiday, Lily seems
harder and more frivolous. The tragic irony of the contrast between Lily's distinction of personality and her
choice of inferior company is pointed with superb clarity;
as we have already seen, Selden's consciousness can, when
necessary, take the full weight of the situation:

It was one of those days when she was so handsome that to
be handsome was enough, and all the rest—her graces, her
social felicities, her quickness—seemed the over-flow of a
bounteous nature. But what especially struck him was the
way in which she detached herself, by a hundred undefinable
shades, from the persons who most abounded in her own

style. It was in just such company, the flower and complete expression of the state she aspired to, that the differences came out with special poignancy, her grace cheapening the other women's smartness as her finely-discriminated silences made their chatter dull. The strain of the last hours had restored to her face the deeper eloquence which Selden had lately missed in it, and the bravery of her words to him still fluttered in her voice and eyes. Yes, she was matchless—it was the one word for her; and he could give his admiration the freer play because so little personal feeling remained in it. His real detachment from her had taken place, not at the lurid moment of disenchantment, but now, in the sober after-light of discrimination, where he saw her definitely divided from him by the crudeness of a choice which seemed to deny the very differences he felt in her. It was before him again in its very completeness—the choice in which she was content to rest: in the stupid costiliness of the food and the showy dulness of the talk, in the freedom of speech which never arrived at wit and the freedom of act which never made for romance. The strident setting of the restaurant, in which their table seemed set apart in a special glare of publicity, and the presence at it of little Dabham of the "Riviera Notes," emphasized the ideals of a world in which conspicuousness passed for distinction, and the society column became the roll of fame. [*The House of Mirth*, Bk. II, 3. Quoted by permission.]

It is in fact her final appearance in this world of hollow but still untarnished glory, and Mrs. Dorset's wanton cruelty at this juncture is the kind of unforeseeable accident that might be fatal to anyone with Lily's record of "imprudence," and that exemplifies the ruthlessness of Society towards its victims. Later, to an appropriately contrasted listener, she sums up in these words:

"Dear Gerty, how little imagination you good people have! Why, the beginning was in my cradle, I suppose—in the way I was brought up, and the things I was taught to care for. Or no—I won't blame anybody for my faults: I'll say it was in my blood, that I got it from some wicked pleasure-loving ancestress, who reacted against the homely virtues of New Amsterdam, and wanted to be back at the court of the

Charleses!" And as Miss Farish continued to press her with troubled eyes, she went on impatiently: "You asked me just now for the truth—well, the truth about any girl is that once she's talked about she's done for; and the more she explains her case the worse it looks.—My good Gerty, you don't happen to have a cigarette about you?" [*The House of Mirth,* Bk. II, 4. Quoted by permission.]

They are a further brilliant expression of the theme of fate, of the social divergencies of the book, and of Lily's character—clear-sighted, sincere, and nonchalant.

When the pharasaical millionaires turn aside from her, it is appropriate that the scandalous Mrs. Fisher should be more generous; she has the simple generosity that is traditionally associated with such people. She finds Lily "employment" organizing the social life of the Sam Gormers, the latest aspirants to fashionable recognition. Lily is from now on definitely outside Society, as it was understood, and her descent is indicated by the sequence of names with whose bearers she is associated; they are one of Edith Wharton's nicest comic touches and, if the seriousness of her perceptiveness and sense of values needs demonstration, we get it when Lily makes comparisons:

The Gormer *milieu* represented a social outskirt which Lily had always fastidiously avoided; but it struck her, now that she was in it, as only a flamboyant copy of her own world, a caricature approximating the real thing as the "society play" approaches the manners of the drawing-room. The people about her were doing the same things as the Trenors, the Van Osburghs and the Dorsets; the difference lay in a hundred shades of aspect and manner, from the pattern of the men's waistcoats to the inflection of the women's voices. Everything was pitched in a higher key, and there was more of each thing: more noise, more color, more champagne, more familiarity—but also greater good-nature, less rivalry, and a fresher capacity for enjoyment. [*The House of Mirth,* Bk. II, 5. Quoted by permission.]

These are the author's reflections as well as the heroine's, and one sees that she not only belonged to a social group that antedated the Four Hundred, but that, as a free intelligence, she could also place critically the whole social structure by such simple human standards as must underlie any manners and customs worth consideration. In the desperate circumstances a rapprochement between Lily and Rosedale is just plausible. He has reached almost the desiderated heights by his own efforts and she now wonders wistfully whether she could persuade him to marry her for love "now that he [has] no other reason." We are about to witness another of those extraordinary displays of highmindedness and foolhardiness in rapid succession which have characterized her before, and the next two sections of the novel are built up on a complex pattern of irony. Lily refuses a chance of revenge on her enemy, Mrs. Dorset, and then almost at once does something fatally reckless in the worldly sense and shockingly cheap morally; she offers herself to Rosedale. Far from accepting for love, he laughs at the offer, but later says he will have her on condition that she completes his social ascent by straightforward blackmail of the same lady. Lily again refuses the opportunity of revenge, although it would also have brought financial salvation. From one point of view, one might call it as fatally stupid a mistake as her offer of marriage at the beginning of the scene; from another, one sees that it is one of the occasions when Lily Bart emerges from her social setting as a tragic heroine.

The final tragic movement, direct or ironical, has now been established firmly, and Lily is shown, little over a year since the glamorous beginning of the book, living in an inferior hotel in New York, completely alone except for the intense and rather uncomprehending Gerty Farish and pursued by "horrors" in her nights of insomnia. She touches her lowest level socially by taking a job as "secretary" to Mrs. Norma Hatch, resident at the Emporium Hotel. Mrs. Hatch's name is the last in the sequence, and everything is thematically appropriate: she lives in a strange under-world of luxury that has no conventions and no routine, not even mealtimes. Edith Wharton was to use this indication of social anarchy even more tellingly twenty and again thirty years later. More so than the Gormer milieu, it is an almost phantasmagoric parody of Society life. Lily's unsuccessful attempts to work in a fashionable milliner's, her lack of the skill complementary to her chief interest in life, is a touching and also profound piece of symbolism. By early spring she is walking the streets to kill time. The symbolism is again both obvious and tragically painful; Lily Bart, who was once warned not to look like a "scarlet woman" at dinner might now look to the ignorant like an ordinary prostitute; it is both pathos and poetic justice. The last scenes show the finer side of Lily uppermost, and we see her looking back over her career with a clarity of vision that indicates again her intelligence, as well as expressing her agony of mind:

> She had learned by experience that she had neither the aptitude nor the moral constancy to remake her life on new lines; to become a worker among workers, and let the world of luxury and pleasure sweep by her unregarded. She could not hold herself much to blame for this ineffectiveness, and she was perhaps less to blame than she believed. Inherited tendencies had combined with early training to make her the highly specialized product she was: an organism as helpless out of its narrow range as the sea-anemone torn from the rock. She had been fashioned to adorn and delight; to what other end does nature round the rose-leaf and paint the humming-bird's breast? And was it her fault that the purely decorative mission is less easily and harmoniously fulfilled among social beings than in the world of nature? That it is apt to be hampered by material necessities or complicated by moral scruples? [*The House of Mirth*, Bk. II, 11. Quoted by permission.]

In both content and phrasing the blending of Lily Bart's reflections and the author's interpretation of the situation is at this point especially harmonious; it would be crass to

boggle at the rhetorical questions. We know that by now
Lily can see nearly everything that her creator sees and it
is this steadily deepening self-awareness and social perceptiveness which, along with her fundamental moral integrity and dignity, give her ultimately her tragic stature.
They have been growing throughout the book, in step
with the deterioration of her circumstances. This is the
tragic pattern and the words in fact take us back forcibly
to Selden's reflections at their opening meeting in New
York eighteen months before. The "moral scruples" that
have all along interfered with her single-minded pursuit of
material comforts are that "fineness" which Selden then
saw. Selden is now portrayed as sympathetic and indeed
touched, but, his temperament being what it is, incapable
of recapturing his old feeling for her, and his behavior
has an inevitability in the circumstances that makes it
seem like a further manifestation of her destiny. Lily
realizes the situation and, after a touchingly elegant gesture of self-dramatization, she sums up for them both:

> "Do you remember what you said to me once? That you
> could help me only by loving me? Well—you did love me for
> a moment; and it helped me. It has always helped me. But
> the moment is gone—it was I who let it go. And one must go
> on living. Good-bye." [*The House of Mirth*, Bk. II, 12.
> Quoted by permission.]

The gesture combines the personal and pathetic frankness
of Lily Bart at the end of her tether with the poise of her
training; it must be said that, cruelly as Society has treated
her, her manner would not have been the same without
its ideals of deportment.

Before the end, Edith Wharton introduces a scene that
few novelists would succeed with. She brings Lily into contact with a working-class girl who is happily married and
a mother; the contrast is obvious but is free from sentimental appeals; it is simply the ironic juxtaposition of

values and circumstances. The sense of finality is very
skillfully evoked; Lily returns to her room and sorts out
from her wardrobe the relics of her past glory and as, by a
coincidence that nevertheless is not obtrusive, a legacy ar-
rives, she is able at least to liquidate the past. Her death
is, however, accidental. Suicide would have been cheap
and sensational, a rescue sentimental; the final irony, characteristic in every way, of Selden's coming to propose to
her and finding her dead is achieved with perfect tact.
Edith Wharton's interest in the Eumenides does not lead
her to introduce any concepts such as "the President of the
Immortals," and indeed the restrained handling of these
last scenes is a triumph of art. The tragedy of Lily Bart
is in many ways the opposite of that of James's tragedy
of Isabel Archer. Isabel has lofty ideals but knows too
little of life to look in the right places for their manifestations and is consequently hopelessly deceived. Lily Bart's
ideals are debased by the influence of her upbringing and
surroundings and she is too sophisticated to look in the
right places for happiness. What were then considered her
lapses would pass unnoticed today, but in any case "indiscretion" would be unnecessary. She would succeed in
earning a good income in some more marginal department
of the hatshop and be an ornament of the smartest cocktail
parties as well. Indeed, a very few years later her tragedy
would have been impossible. But it is no less a tragedy for
its exact period setting. As Edith Wharton says in her
preface, it is such details that give vividness to a novel.
She has in turn succeeded in giving these details lasting
interest from the situation, and made a tragic novel
subtler than Hardy's study of purity of motive among simpler people and more directly moving than James's tragedy
of cosmopolitan life.

II

Edith Wharton did not heed the plea of Charles Eliot

Norton to remember that "no great work of the imagination has ever been based on illicit passion."[3] Both of the
tragedies of high life that followed *The House of Mirth*, in
so far as they can be classified as tragedies, have to some
extent that basis. Neither of these works, however, has
its depth and range; there is a conflict between the individual and conventional social values, but in both cases it
is decidedly, and rather curiously, restricted—in *Madame de Treymes*, 1907, to a small Franco-American
group in the Faubourg St.-Germain and in *The Reef*,
1912, to an American group in a country château. The
latter book thus seems, as it were, doubly isolated and
insulated; there is no real surrounding community even
implied, and the advocacy of French aristocratic conventions by the American-born Marquise is intended to
be ridiculous. Both books suffer a little from over-
"doing" in the Jamesian sense. Whereas *The House of
Mirth* is a worthy successor to James's work, these books
owe rather too much to him. James, who greatly admired *The Reef* for its delocalized quality and also for its
dramatic structure, compared it to *Bérénice*,[4] though it is
difficult to see how one can do this except by arbitrarily
shifting the center of the plot.

Madame de Treymes bears an obvious resemblance to
James's *The American*. It appeared in *Scribner's* in 1906,
the year before he republished his novel with a Preface
in the New York Edition, and one wonders whether he
could have been in any way affected by her treatment of
the subject; he expresses admiration in a letter.[5] At all
events she seems to anticipate his view that *The American*
is too much of a romance and to show, in her story, a more
"general sense of 'the way things happen.'" She takes his

---

3. *A Backward Glance*, p. 127.
4. *The Letters*, 2: 370.
5. *Ibid.* p. 57. Leon Edel tells me that he knows of no other reference
   in James's letter and thinks any influence unlikely.

basic situation, brings it up to date, complicates it, and, in so doing, treats it more realistically. Instead of the simple-minded Newman, Edith Wharton presents us with the francophile New Yorker, Durham, who is as sophisticated in his own way as the French aristocracy and who feels a gently pitying contempt for his relatives. He meets again Fanny de Malrive (née Frisbee), who has made an unhappy marriage but, though separated from her husband, has stayed on in Paris to bring up her son. Madame de Treymes, who is the intermediary between Durham and the Malrives in trying to arrange for an actual divorce, is a brilliantly created character who does indeed make the typical Americans seem crude and gawky. The background is all done with tremendous care and appropriateness, especially the different houses of the Faubourg; the relationship between the French and the Americans is symbolized most fittingly in the organization of "ventes de charité" by inhabitants of the Faubourg, at which Americans spend vast sums of money in the hope of getting in return an invitation to tea.

Durham and Madame de Treymes are well matched in conversational skill for the complicated bargaining that is worked out between them. One first sees a simple clash of moral principles between all that she and Durham stand for, though they themselves are at one in manners and taste. This is followed by more subtle moves and countermoves, until she is so impressed by his standard of honor that she reveals the utter duplicity of the family, and the story ends with a scene of personal confession by Madame de Treymes and renunciation by Durham in the mode of high comedy of manners but with implications of tragedy. Thus in the confrontation of ideals there is no straight contrast of the acceptable and the unacceptable, as there is in James's novel. The Malrives are the proud and wicked foreign nobles believing only in the family and the Church, but they are also out for any material aid they can get, as James, in his Preface, says such people would be; Madame de Treymes may be, as she says herself, "false to the core," but she feels deeply for Durham and Fanny in terms of personal happiness. Durham, with all his conversational wit and social polish, has his unshakable standard of truth that makes him sacrifice his own happiness, and, perhaps one might say, the greater part of Fanny's. This is tragic irony of a solemn kind.

Madame de Treymes is a *nouvelle* in scale and, making all allowances, one feels that it is nevertheless rather too much a period piece and a literary exercise. *The Reef* is more substantial. It could be classed as an ironic tragedy like *The House of Mirth* in that the finer qualities of the heroine contribute as much to the unhappy conclusion as do her weaknesses. The tragedy of Anna Leath is that of a woman, over-fastidious by nature and so molded by social training that she cannot face the realities of life. The book is also the tragedy of Sophy Viner, an independent American girl who has had to make her own way in the world without background or resources—a less sophisticated and socially inferior Lily Bart. The pattern is much more formal than in *The House of Mirth;* it is arranged, after the manner of a tragic drama, in five books, with contrasting scenes and with past history skillfully dovetailed into the current narrative.

Book I opens with George Darrow, an American diplomat and man of the world, though remarkably lacking in any kind of national characteristics, about to renew contact with Anna at her Chateau de Givré; he becomes involved in Paris with Sophy Viner, and this temporary alliance of worldliness and genuinely innocent emancipation has many later ramifications; Sophy says that it "was the only chance [she has] ever had," and the final incident of the unopened letter from Anna suggests that it means more to Darrow than he later admits to himself.

At all events the limitations of Darrow's kind of worldly experience in terms of real understanding of himself and of other people, even his own countrywomen, have already become apparent. Book II is constructed to make a strongly contrasted impression. We are now shown Givré, with its terraces and park glowing in October sunlight, and Anna Leath waiting for Darrow in a mood of blissful confidence. She is now "done" at full length for us and we realize how tied and sheltered she has always been and how little inclined by nature to break loose. We learn that she was brought up in a world where "people with emotion were not visited," that she discouraged Darrow in his youth, when he was "tall, fair and easy," by wanting to talk about books when he wanted to kiss her. Instead she married Fraser Leath, a gallicized American of the Gilbert Osmond type, whose kiss was like a "cold smooth pebble." In contrast again is her stepson, the gay and impulsive Owen Leath and, when they meet, her running to greet him represents a revival of youthful feeling. Despite their differences, they feel themselves fellow-rebels against the weight of the French aristocratic tradition that is artificially forced upon them. Anna and Darrow are brought together with all the beauty and refinement of Givré as background. Each is in his own way diplomatic. Their exchanges are diffident and understated—"This is no light thing between us"; they have the shyness and reticence of two people with separate lives behind them, but each is delighted with the other, and, despite the element of worldliness in him, Darrow feels that "it's the best thing that has ever happened to [him] anyhow." Darrow and Anna Leath have on their hands, in very different ways, the crucial problem of Owen's marriage. For Anna it is a matter of dealing with American and French moral and social conventions, in the person of her mother-in-law, the Marquise de Chantelle. For Darrow the problem is that the girl is

Sophy Viner, who is at Givré as governess to Anna's own daughter.

He does not actually discover that Sophy is Owen's prospective fiancée until well on in Book III, and there is something a little theatrical in the pejorative sense in the way this revelation is delayed and also in the way that Owen is made to feel suspicious of Darrow's relations with Sophy at about the same time. Though Darrow no longer feels any personal interest in Sophy, he opposes the marriage from a quite mistaken interpretation of her as an adventuress, and tells her, with what one later discovers is complex irony: "You'll be wretched if you marry a man you're not in love with." The problem is solved temporarily by the arrival of the Marquise's confidante, Adelaide Painter, who pronounces the match an "old-fashioned American case, as sweet and sound as home-made bread," and a double betrothal is celebrated. The episode represents an intrusion of comic—rather too comic—provinciality upon solemn sophistication and the solution is too simple and unrelated to realities; Book IV shows its rapid break-up. By now one realizes that, with her suspicious temperament, it will take more than Darrow's diplomatic skill to restore confidence between himself and Anna. One also now sees the depth of Sophy's tragedy—she could be Bérénice, if one is bent on making the comparison; she only now realizes all the "adventure" has meant to her. She has an absolute sincerity about her own feelings, which puts Darrow again to shame; he has remembered her foolish limitations as much as her charm. Anna now becomes fully the "jealous woman" she admits she is, and one sees a feline watchfulness in her that is the reverse of her naivety. Darrow is beaten in his efforts to convince her of the insignificance of the affair for him, and Sophy confirms all her suspicions with the supreme simplicity of "I wanted it—I chose it. He was good to me." Anna cannot cope with what she considers the horror of the affair and her situation is summed up in the admission to herself, "I shall never know what that girl has known." In the context this is a powerful and complex understatement; Anna Leath in fact lacks the emotional capacity for such knowledge in any circumstances.

Anna's tragedy drags itself out through one more Book, accentuated by nervous shuttling between Givré and Paris. She cannot separate the Darrow she loves from the Darrow she abhors and she is obsessed by deceit on all sides. However, when Darrow tries to make her see that they can patch things up on a basis of mutual understanding she begins, though she cannot see this, to realize her own weakness:

> All through these meditations ran the undercurrent of an absolute trust in Sophy Viner. She thought of the girl with a mingling of antipathy and confidence. It was humiliating to her pride to recognize kindred impulses in a character which she would have liked to feel completely alien to her. But what indeed was the girl really like? She seemed to have no scruples and a thousand delicacies. She had given herself to Darrow, and concealed the episode from Owen Leath, with no more apparent sense of debasement than the vulgarest of adventuresses; yet she had instantly obeyed the voice of her heart when it bade her part from the one and serve the other. [Edith Wharton, *The Reef*, Charles Scribner's Sons, Bk. V, 33. Copyright 1912 Edith Wharton; renewal copyright 1940 William R. Tyler. Quoted by permission.]

Anna's tragedy is that she cannot obey "the voice of her heart" and she realizes now that she was "cold" to her first husband. This may be ironical as far as he is concerned, but it takes up a number of earlier suggestions to indicate that she lacks just that strength of impulse which might have swept aside conventional prejudices and personal reservations and drawn her to accept her relationship with Darrow as it is. As Edith Wharton puts it, "she was one of those luckless women who always have the wrong audacities and who always know it." Through a series of tense and vivid scenes she wavers between accepting Darrow and giving him up; she nags on and on to the verge of hysteria, when he gives her what at this point looks like his final answer with its implied comment:

> She continued to gaze at him through tear-dilated eyes; and suddenly she flung out the question: "Wasn't it the Athenée you took her to that evening?"
>
> "Anna—Anna."
>
> "Yes; I want to know now: to know everything. Perhaps that will make me forget. I ought to have made you tell me before. Wherever we go, I imagine you've been there with her . . . I see you together. I want to know how it began, where you went, why you left her . . . I can't go on in this darkness any longer!"
>
> She did not know what had prompted her passionate outburst, but already she felt lighter, freer, as if at last the evil spell were broken. "I want to know everything," she repeated. "It's the only way to make me forget."
>
> After she had ceased speaking Darrow remained where he was, his arms folded, his eyes lowered, immovable. She waited, her gaze on his face.
>
> "Aren't you going to tell me?"
>
> "No."
>
> The blood rushed to her temples. "You won't? Why not?"
>
> "If I did, do you suppose you'd forget *that?*"
>
> "Oh—" she moaned, and turned away from him.
>
> "You see it's impossible," he went on. "I've done a thing I loathe, and to atone for it you ask me to do another. What sort of satisfaction would that give you? It would put something irremediable between us."
>
> She leaned her elbow against the mantel-shelf and hid her face in her hands. She had the sense that she was vainly throwing away her last hope of happiness, yet she could do nothing, think of nothing to save it. The conjecture flashed through her: "Should I be at peace if I gave him up?" and she remembered the desolation of the days after she had sent him away, and understood that that hope was vain. The tears welled through her lids and ran slowly down between her fingers.
>
> "Good-bye," she heard him say, and his footsteps turned to the door. [*The Reef*, Bk. V, 38. Quoted by permission.]

Darrow's moral stature has been growing as hers has

declined, and he ends with a dignified repentance as well as an implied condemnation of her.

The ending is open. We are left with mere possibilities, none of them "happy," let alone exalting in the full tragic sense. Sophy, in a way, comes off best. She demonstrates a simple integrity that has so far survived a sordid background, but her prospects are not propitious. By contrast, Anna Leath, with all her advantages of culture, is left in total disarray. If she is to be united with Darrow, it will be only on the basis of some kind of compromise similar to the ending of *The Letters*, written a few years before.

Summarized in this way, the novel may seem excessively schematic and rather lifeless, and in fact it does lack vitality, except in Sophy Viner. Even Darrow is not a strongly felt presence. He has his rather unpleasant egotistical side and it is difficult to imagine how even Sophy failed to notice it, but, assuming that she did not and leaving aside the way he took her to the Paris theaters, one still cannot see how he made such an impression on her. Until the end, when he gets exasperated with Anna, he is very much the conventional upper-class type who might turn up anywhere between the Hudson and the Urals before 1914.

Anna herself, whether intentionally or not, is a portrait of the sort of qualities that militate against vitality, and her "fineness" seems extremely rarefied. The faded autumnal beauty of Givré, while it has its suitability for the revival of a love affair in middle age, certainly does not do much to suggest a revival of passion. The book decidedly shows the danger of dispensing with what Edith Wharton herself calls "the unrolling social picture"; James was wrong to admire this aspect. Consideration of Anna Leath as a tragic heroine raises grave doubts. One seems meant to sympathize with her and to regret her jealous tendencies, but the fineness that Darrow admires is so lacking in human warmth, apart from her devotion to

Owen, so narrow in sympathy and so prudish for a middle-aged woman, even allowing for her cloistered milieu and for the reticences of the time, that it is almost impossible to accept it as a value. If one cannot so sympathize and regret, then there ceases to be any ironical interplay between the two sides of her character, and running to meet Owen represents all the independence she is capable of. This, of course, is an exaggeration as much as the opposite estimate, but it is doubtful whether her career can be considered a tragedy, even in the sense that Sophy Viner's story is tragic in its humble way. The absence of a rich social background to give solidity to the main themes makes us feel that Anna's fastidiousness and jealousy, and also to some extent Sophy's naivety and Owen's conflict with tradition are all rather preposterous. One does not see enough of the "well-regulated, well-fed . . . world" of Anna's childhood or even the tradition-bound austere world of Givré to make them real. One is expected to be impressed by Anna's inhibited and romanticizing nature and her disillusionment as a theme of high tragedy, only needing, as it were, "drapery"—to refer again to Edith Wharton's preface to the *House of Mirth*—but it is not really possible to respond in this way.

Edith Wharton's attitude to her story is, in any case, not absolutely unambiguous. Sympathy for Anna is clearly intended throughout most of it, but that final scene in Mrs. McTarvie-Birch's bedroom, though one may feel it is a bit overdone in a slapdash commonplace way, nonetheless underlines heavily all the implied criticisms of Anna and seems very seriously to diminish her tragedy without making one any better satisfied with the book as a whole. *The Reef* has become dated. One feels that it is much more a tragedy of 1912 than *The House of Mirth* is a tragedy of 1905. Although James thought so highly of it, Edith Wharton herself repudiated it immediately after publication,[6] not least its autobiographical implications. The central situation appears at first sight rather like her own, but Darrow is not Walter Berry at any time and Leath is certainly not Edward Wharton. There could be memories of Morton Fullerton in Darrow, however, and one could relate various scenes and other characters to the author's life in various ways if one were so disposed. In attempting to sum up one's criticism of the novel, one comes back to one's first impression, its lack of vitality, and one is left thinking how strange it is that, as Anna Leath seems undoubtedly a partial critical self-portrait, the book lacks strength of feeling in this way. Possibly Edith Wharton was too intent on distancing the sources of her material, which would in turn underline the implicit self-criticism in the character of Anna Leath.

---

6. See Lewis, *op. cit.*, p. 326.

4 Tragedy in Middle-Class Life

I

When one talks of snobbery in Mrs. Wharton, one should remember that, though her last novel is about a duchess, her first published short story is set in very low middle-class New York, and that both *Ethan Frome,* 1911, her most famous short novel, and also *Summer,* 1917, belong to village life in New England. Even though she may not really have known much about America west of the Hudson, Edith Wharton knew a good deal about life just above the manual-worker level—and below that level also —nearer her own homes, and her knowledge dates from very early life. It was not something she deliberately acquired as a literary duty, and, more important, she made great literature out of it. *Mrs. Manstey's View* was written when she was under thirty. It is known that *Bunner Sisters,* though not published till 1916, was drafted at about the same time;[1] *Ethan Frome* dates from about 1907. She did not reprint *Mrs. Manstey,*[2] but it is not negligible; it is a pathetic little tragedy of the extinction of a simple soul's last interest.

It may be questioned whether these stories are in any sense tragic. Lionel Trilling has described characters of this type as people who merely exist; *Ethan Frome* is, he

---

1. Blake Nevius quotes a reference to the story from a letter to Edward Burlingame, editor of *Scribner's Magazine,* dated 25 November 1893 (*Edith Wharton,* p. 253).
2. See *Scribner's Magazine* 10 (July 1891).

says, "a story about people who do not make moral deci-
sions,[3] but are helpless victims of circumstance, contrived
by the author, and go on living by mere inertia. This is
probably truer of *Ethan Frome* than of the other two, but
there is indeed a general absence of social conflict, with its
complexities and ironies, except in *Summer*, though here
the chief character is an outcast rather than a rebel and
society is represented as uncompromisingly hostile. In all
three disaster comes with a terrible inevitability to small
lives. One thinks at once of George Eliot's earlier stories;
and a great deal of Barbara Hardy's discussion of these
as "unheroic tragedy" is relevant to Edith Wharton's
work.[4] These stories show a much drearier way of life than
that of the English Midlands and present to us humble
heroes of quite as "limited emotional capacity," undevel-
oped intelligence, and unawakened imagination as Amos
Barton's or Silas Marner's. Edith Wharton ranges more
freely than George Eliot in her choice of subject matter,
but none of her chief characters is a complex personality.
She was decidedly engaged in extending the sympathies
of her fashionable contemporary readers by showing them
the pathetically commonplace and the grimly frustrated.
She gives her situations emotional intensity and significance and her characters what Mrs. Hardy calls "aesthetic
stiffening" by the strength of her dramatization, by rigor-
ous economy in the selection of detail, and by a clear,
restrained, and concrete prose style; she condemned *Scenes
from Clerical Life* as very ill-written.[5] Mrs. Hardy's final
comment on George Eliot's early work might be even more
fittingly applied to these stories:

In the world of her narrative and in its human units we find

---

3. "The Morality of Inertia" in *A Gathering of Fugitives*, London: Secker,
1957.
4. *The Novels of George Eliot*, London: The Athlone Press, 1959, Chapter
1.
5. Review of Leslie Stephen's *George Eliot* in *The Bookman* 15, 1902.

the free life of realistic fiction at its best—free even to show
the undramatic and unromantic bits of life—but organized
by the intense and driving emphasis of formative vision.

From the intensity of the vision springs the tragic feeling.
These are not great tragedies but, as regards both the individual and the representative quality of the protagonists,
limited presentations of suffering; they are cases of "as
flies to wanton boys . . ." with the gods in the remote
background. They evoke pity and fear, if no exaltation.

II

Bunner Sisters belongs to a small world, a corner of old
New York that is most clearly and precisely visualized.
The precarious balance on "the extreme verge of gentility," to use E. M. Forster's phrase,[6] is indicated by the fact
that the sisters' basement shop has the only really clean
window in the street. It is a tragedy of inexperience, of the
most naïve romanticizing, and of shattering disillusionment. The sisters have very limited desires and aspirations,
overlaid by small pious conventions. They lack any kind
of sophistication or discrimination except a pathetic little
snobbery. So far from being socially rebellious, they cling
desperately to their bottom rung of the middle-class ladder
and look up reverently to their one anonymous customer
from "the Square." Everything in the opening scene, from
the carefully listed and described contents of the bed-sitter
behind the shop to the half-educated dialogue, contrib-
utes to the impression of the humblest refinements, barely
maintained. Their best silk dresses have been "made over"
more than once. The acquisition of a cheap clock is a
major extravagance. The introduction of an emotional
complication in the shape of a German clock-seller into
their lives is done with delicately comic irony. We are

6. *Howard's End*, London: Arnold, 1532, p. 43.

given a contrast between the sentimental speculations and the futile stratagem of the elder sister, Ann Eliza, and the more impulsive behavior of the younger, Evelina; the childish guile they employ toward each other has its counterpart in childlike innocence toward the rest of the world and Mr. Ramy in particular. Even the full-blooded melodramatic fantasy-building of the dressmaker, Miss Mellins, shows up their pathetic lack of experience. One sees considerable possibilities of both sinister motive and gullibility in the ambiguities of:

". . . And I don't believe he's forty; but he *does* look sick. I guess he's pretty lonesome, all by himself in that store. He as much as told me so, and somehow"—Evelina paused and bridled—"I kinder thought that maybe his saying he'd call round about the clock was on'y just an excuse. He said it just as I was going out of the store. What you think, Ann Eliza?" [Edith Wharton, "Bunner Sisters," in *Xingu and Other Stories*, Charles Scribner's Sons. Copyright 1916 Edith Wharton; renewal copyright 1944 William R. Tyler. Quoted by permission.]

Mr. Ramy is not, however, an active villain; he merely exploits an opportunity that is thrust upon him. He represents an inevitable intrusion by society rather than an attack; moral isolationism proves impossible in the face of natural impulses on both sides.

The next stage of the story produces its main effect by ironical counterpoint. The more deeply Mr. Ramy establishes himself in the confidence of the sisters, the more dubious his character appears to the reader. His unprepossessing appearance does not trouble their sex-starved natures and Evelina "creates" for herself a series of new bonnets. Even the pointed remarks of a friend on his illness arouse no suspicion. The most touchingly ironical episode occurs when, contrary to all expectations, he proposes to the elder sister. She does not notice his sheer opportunism and though she refuses him with composure,

we are made to realize that it is indeed the great experience of her life. His proposal "after a decent interval" to
Evelina in no way detracts from her own feeling of fulfillment, which now blends into a vicarious sharing in
Evelina's exultation. It is obvious by now that the sisters
are lost in a world of sentimental illusions that is a product
of their restricted circumstances and their absorption in
each other. They are not even capable of judging by appearances, let alone perceiving any underlying realities.
The elder and professedly more responsible Ann Eliza,
whose is the registering consciousness throughout, is as
completely taken in as her sister. The whole psychological
situation is most penetratingly analyzed. The slightly vulgar wedding scene represents a climax of intrusion into
the closed world as well as its break-up.

The nature of the cruel fate and attendant suffering
that the Bunner sisters have brought upon themselves
through no positive fault of their own is revealed as a
double ordeal, spiritual as well as material. For the elder
it begins as solitude:

> The whole aspect of the place had changed with the changed
> conditions of Ann Eliza's life. The first customer who opened
> the shop-door startled her like a ghost; and all night she lay
> tossing on her side of the bed, sinking now and then into an
> uncertain doze from which she would suddenly wake to reach
> out her hand for Evelina. In the new silence surrounding her
> the walls and furniture found voice, frightening her at dusk
> and midnight with strange sighs and stealthy whispers.
> Ghostly hands shook the window shutters or rattled at the
> outer latch, and once she grew cold at the sound of a step
> like Evelina's stealing through the dark shop to die out on
> the threshold. In time, of course, she found an explanation
> for these noises, telling herself that the bedstead was warping,
> that Miss Mellins trod heavily overhead, or that the thunder
> of passing beer-waggons shook the door-latch; but the hours
> leading up to these conclusions were full of the floating
> terrors that harden into fixed foreboding. ["Bunner Sisters,"
> in *Xingu and Other Stories*. Quoted by permission.]

By such discreetly heightened rendering of the movements
of Ann Eliza's consciousness Edith Wharton once or twice
adds powerfully to the impact of actual episodes. Solitude
is soon exacerbated by loss of postal contact—Evelina's
high-falutin' letters belong in any case to the world of
illusion—and helpless searching for an address, as pathetic
as a search for an actual person. This eventually leads to
her discovery, in pathetically ironical circumstances, that
her sister has married a drug addict. Physical illness and
increasing poverty are added to mental suffering. Evelina's
ordeal is similar and more immediately and overwhelm-
ingly painful. Her blunt statement, " 'I've been to hell and
back'," represents utter disillusionment for both of them
and is substantiated in terms of material degradation and
mental torture; she has ended by begging in the streets.
Ann Eliza raises her up again just above the verge of gentility by not allowing her to die in a hospital; the indignity
of a public hospital is the last surviving delusion, and indication of their social ethos. The more adventurous and
self-regarding sister has experienced more of life and a
fuller disillusionment, which actually leads her to a measure of simple wisdom and serenity in the Catholic Church,
though it should be mentioned that the cost of the funeral
finally ruins Ann Eliza; the irony here has several levels.
The last scene on a spring morning is contrasted with the
preceding gloom but "the stir of innumerable beginnings"
accentuates Ann Eliza's destitution; she has nothing left
but her self-respect and her courage. Herein may perhaps
be found a moral drama underlying the tragic sequence of
events. If there is any positive moral error it is in Evelina's
innocent egotism before her marriage; she has always, for
example, accepted the larger piece of pie. Ann Eliza is
shown rather as indifferent to self, a kind of negative
virtue; there are signs at the end, however, of a new independence of character, if not of condition. Nevertheless
the disaster is almost annihilating, and one cannot feel

that she is capable of much more than survival. The victims of upbringing and environment have been put through a horrible purgation and even the survivor is almost exhausted. She has gained indeed very little more than the moral strength of inertia. However one takes the ending, there can be no doubt about the depth of Edith Wharton's compassion, as it is shown there, nor about her sympathetic handling of the wretched details of the story. She kept her critical irony for vulgarians on much higher income levels.

III

It is not surprising that *Ethan Frome* has been overpraised, though it is strange that it has caught more attention than *Summer*. Edith Wharton has told us about the early draft in French and about her joy in producing the final version under Walter Berry's exacting scrutiny:

> For years I had wanted to draw life as it really was in the derelict mountain villages of New England, a life even in my time, and a thousandfold more a generation earlier, utterly unlike that seen through the rose-coloured spectacles of my predecessors, Mary Wilkins and Sarah Orne Jewett. In those days the snow-bound villages of Western Massachusetts were still grim places, morally and physically: insanity, incest and slow mental and moral starvation were hidden away behind the paintless wooden house-fronts of the long village street, or in the isolated farm-houses on the neighbouring hills; and Emily Brontë would have found as savage tragedies in our remoter valleys as on her Yorkshire moors. [*A Backward Glance*, Chap. XII. Quoted by permission.]

The story is especially closely written, the narrator being made to assume the role of editor; he says he coordinates, which is perhaps a better expression, as he produces a continuous story and not a collection of anecdotes, which might at first sight have been more naturalistic;

Edith Wharton had, however, carefully thoughtout reasons in terms of both subject and story-telling technique for using the method she borrowed from Balzac's *La Grande Bretêche*.[7] Within his role, the narrator is the omniscient author; he interprets what he has been told; no one could have told him some of the details that he puts into his "vision." The name Starkfield is all too suitable for the remote Massachusetts village, and the landscape is as carefully chosen as any of Hardy's. One is not made strongly aware of the religious background as a body of doctrine but one has a sense of a narrow world, whose foundations are religious, closing in on the inhabitants and of poverty, sickness, and inescapable unhappiness. Only little breakaways at rare intervals are possible; it is appropriate to the place as well as to Puritan tradition that Endurance has been a women's name. The opening sentence sets the tone; it is informal, businesslike, and utterly detached:

> I had the story, bit by bit, from various people, and, as generally happens in such cases, each time it was a different story. [Edith Wharton, *Ethan Frome*, Charles Scribner's Sons. Copyright 1911 Edith Wharton; renewal copyright 1939 William R. Tyler. Quoted by permission.]

The implication is, as Edith Wharton wished to suggest, of rural inarticulateness and exasperating inconsequence, which the narrator has ordered and disciplined. One is then confronted with Frome, "the ruin of a man," crippled by an accident, and one infers the existence of a hypochondriac wife; " '. . . he's been in Starkfield too many winters. . . . Most of the smart ones get away.' " sums up the two basic features of the scene and its influence, the numbing rather than bracing cold and the difficulty of communications. Frome, however, is not a clod; he preserves an interest in science from early days at a Technical

---

7. See her Introduction to Scribner's Modern Student's Library edition, 1922.

College. When at the climax of the introductory section the narrator is snowbound at the Frome farm, even the house looks appropriately "stunted" because Frome has pulled down the wing linking it to the farm buildings which, it is said, "seem[s] to be the centre, the actual hearthstone, of a New England farm." The impression that everything has been contrived and the impression of spontaneous happening are just about equally strong, and the plan of the book as a whole, with its carefully arranged flashbacks, accentuates both this more literary quality in a narrow sense and also the essential fatalism. It is a tale of gratuitous and unavoidable frustration of natural impulses, of revolt, and of suffering. There is again no social conflict; human and inanimate environment seem all one. We already know that Ethan Frome has married the cousin who nursed his senile mother. We learn later that Zeena was once a "smart" and lively bride, but she has become both the supreme product and, for Frome, the ever-present representative of that environment, a silent brooding power from which he cannot escape. She represents no one particular oppression, such as Puritan tradition, but the whole range of suspicions, obligations, and restrictions, large and small, that arise in an isolated and impoverished community, stiffened by Calvinism. There is a decided element of caricature in the treatment of Zeena. With "her hard perpendicular bonnet" and the "querulous lines from her thin nose to the corners of her mouth," she appears as the very incarnation of dyspepsia and uncharitableness. We are shown Frome torn between the exacting dominance of this presence and his natural attraction to Mattie Silver, *her* young and destitute cousin—Mattie's story is all of a piece with the rest—who has been brought to help in the house. This domestic situation is cunningly but effectively sandwiched into an account of Ethan Frome fetching the girl back from a dance; the contrast brings out his emotional situation with simple forcefulness. Ref-

erences to Mattie's incompetence and her vague intellectual sympathy add to the sum of "temptations," which
are so inevitable that they seem merely part of his fatal
environment; circumstances, action, sensation, and wish-
ful thinking are clearly and naturally related in the description of their return home:

> For the first time he stole his arm about her, and she did
> not resist. They walked on as if they were floating on a sum-
> mer stream.
> Zeena always went to bed as soon as she had had her
> supper, and the shutterless windows of the house were dark.
> A dead cucumber-vine dangled from the porch like the crape
> streamer tied to the door for a death, and the thought flashed
> through Ethan's brain: "If it was there for Zeena—" Then he
> had a distinct sight of his wife lying in their bedroom asleep,
> her mouth slightly open, her false teeth in a tumbler by
> the bed. [*Ethan Frome*. Quoted by permission.]

When, between the presentation of this situation and
the consequence, Ethan Frome and Mattie are thrown
together, he is totally inhibited by his opportunity, but a
trivial accident results in Mattie's departure in favor of
a "hired girl," which implies financial ruin as well as emotional stagnation for Frome. Zeena's state is summed up
with a grimly comic reference and an ominous suggestion:

> Almost everybody in the neighbourhood had "troubles,"
> frankly localized and specified; but only the chosen had
> "complications." To have them was in itself a distinction,
> though it was also, in most cases, a death-warrant. [*Ethan
> Frome*. Quoted by permission.]

Each succeeding episode increases the feeling of inevitability, and images of small disasters, such as "netted butter-
flies," increase the pathos. Frome forms wild plans for
escaping West with Mattie, until he realizes that he cannot
even afford the fare, and he runs through a gamut of
impulses, including deceit of friends; it is all too primitive

to be called social rebellion. Though the final act is described as "some erratic impulse," one feels that it is the
last of a sequence. The last "coast" down the frozen hill
and the suicide pact that fails are a symbolic culmination,
very powerfully rendered, of the main theme of head-on
frustration. The image of Zeena, obtruded in Frome's
consciousness just before the crash, reminds us of the
theme of infidelity. This is a minor element, however;
there has been no real moral any more than social conflict. Ethan Frome's actions are the product of his environment and his natural temperament and the author does not
blame him; Zeena calls Mattie "a bad girl" for breaking
a plate, but the moral overtone, though implied, is not
very important. One "accident" partly helps them; the
next, their survival, is disastrous.

The epilogue presents a state of death in life and life in
death, the two cripples looked after by the ex-hypochon-
driac in a setting of direst poverty; Zeena has developed
thus far morally. One of the narrator's informants, a
character comparable to Nellie Dean, registers the grim-
ness and the pathos and Frome's surviving pride. There is
no suggestion of either punishment or release, simply of
continuous pain.

It is not difficult to criticize *Ethan Frome*. Despite, indeed perhaps because of, Edith Wharton's skill, one feels
it is a little too inevitable. The contrasts are a little too
sharp, the setting a little too bleak, the characters almost
caricature—of a grim kind, the disaster melodramatic, and
the end unrelievedly wretched. Apart from the formal
derivation from Balzac, the construction and the atmosphere in fact remind one more of Hardy than of Emily
Brontë; the book lacks both the delicacy and the power
of *Wuthering Heights*. One sees a certain kinship between
Frome with his thwarted intellectual ambition and Jude
Fawley. It is a peasant tragedy in an American setting.
Ultimately one probably agrees with Trilling's criticism,

but one must recognize the distinction of the story, as he recognizes the stoic virtues it offers for our admiration, the endurance and self-respect in the face of hopeless odds. It has something of "the bare, sheer, penetrating power" that Arnold attributed to Wordsworth's *Michael* and comparable poems. Insofar as he rebels, Ethan Frome seems to rebel against life itself—as it exists at Starkfield—rather than against vestigial Puritanism or the social system, but his self-respect and independence, preserved at any cost, are fundamental middle-class qualities, masculine equivalents of the Miss Bunners' little gentilities. In both cases tragedy culminates in an all-out assault on these values, the last refuge of the individual, and, limited as the scope it, one feels the ultimate human significance of what is involved in the particular and the class situation. Miss Bunner saves nothing for certain but her self-respect; Ethan Frome keeps his economic independence also, but in conditions that almost nullify it. Edith Wharton has recorded certain social facts, the resignation and pathetic conservatism, the personal pride and desperate individualism of a large number of people of a certain type and class background. She invites us to admire, but to realize the misery to which devotion to these values may lead. Her picture does not fit into any version of the class struggle except as an embarrassing problem, but one should be grateful to her for showing it, as one is to her for showing that tragedy is possible also among the merely well-to-do.

IV

Summer has a larger scope. It rises a little higher in the middle-class scale and it sinks far below it into the abyss of poverty. Her account of its genesis is joined with that of *Ethan Frome* when she says:

. . . every detail about the colony of drunken mountain out-

laws described in "Summer" was given to me by the rector
of the church at Lenox (near which we lived), and that the
lonely peak I have called "the Mountain" was in reality Bear
Mountain, an isolated summit not more than twelve miles
from our own home. The rector had been fetched there by
one of the mountain outlaws to read the Burial Service over
a woman of evil reputation; and when he arrived every one
in the house of mourning was drunk, and the service was
performed as I have related it . . .

Needless to say, when "Summer" appeared, this chapter was
received with indignant denial by many reviewers and readers;
and not the least vociferous were the New Englanders who
had for years sought the reflection of local life in the rose-and-
lavender pages of their favourite authoresses—and had forgotten to look into Hawthorne's. [*A Backward Glance,* Chap.
XII. Quoted by permission.]

What she got from the parson and what was based on more
immediate experience Edith Wharton made into a very
remarkable book.[8] Strictly speaking, one should not perhaps call it a tragedy. It ends in the marriage of the
heroine, but the circumstances of the marriage are grim
indeed and high romantic hopes have been betrayed and
disappointed. If one has to have a name, ironic tragi-
comedy probably describes the mode best. It is Edith
Wharton's extreme case of the conflict of the individual
with society. Where the Miss Bunners and Ethan Frome
struggle to keep a position, Charity Royall struggles to
establish human relationships of any kind, and to get into
human society at all. She is the child of a drunken convict
and a whore, who has been rescued from a community—
if so anarchic a gathering can be thus described—of outlaws. With her small swarthy face, she has for the cis-
Atlantic reader the classic gipsy appearance and is in fact
once or twice referred to by that term. She begins as the

---

8. It is interesting that in the 30s a film company found *Summer* "too
immoral" for the screen. See Loren Carroll, "Profile of Edith Wharton,"
The Herald Tribune, European Edition, 16 November, 1936.

absolute outsider, hating, as she says, everything, only happy in communion with the natural scene:

> She was blind and insensible to many things, and dimly knew it; but to all that was light and air, perfume and colour, every drop of blood in her responded. She loved the roughness of the dry mountain grass under her palms, the smell of the thyme into which she crushed her face, the fingering of the wind in her hair and through her cotton blouse, and the creak of the larches as they swayed to it. [Edith Wharton, *Summer*, Charles Scribner's Sons. Copyright 1917 Edith Wharton. Quoted by permission.]

She appears as a child of nature as well as a natural child; besides being naturally virtuous, sensitive, and unsophisticated, she can be obstinate and willful, and sometimes spiteful and even violent. She has reason to hope that she may enter society on her own terms, and in the course of her romantic experience and her disillusionment her character unfolds and deepens. She ends by accepting and being accepted into the village. "Things don't change at North Dormer, people just get used to them," she says at the beginning, and her words carry more meaning than she realizes. This is the moral and emotional pattern. It is worked out with decided economy but with more richness and complexity than in its two predecessors, and one appreciates the justice of Edith Wharton's own comment that she did not remember "ever visualizing with more intensity the inner scene, or the creatures peopling it."

Charity Royall is pitted against another isolated, grim, and ingrown fragment of New England. The physical scene is less bleak than at Starkfield and indeed has an idyllic quality to which Charity is, as has been shown, attuned, but it is overshadowed by the Mountain, where the outlaws live and which represents barbarity and primitive degeneracy, and North Dormer is a poor and decaying village. Charity's position there is summarized at an early stage:

Poor and ignorant as she was, and knew herself to be—humblest of the humble even in North Dormer, where to come from the Mountain was the worst disgrace—yet in her narrow world she had always ruled. It was partly, of course, owing to the fact that Lawyer Royall was the "biggest man" in North Dormer; so much too big for it, in fact, that outsiders, who didn't know, always wondered how it held him. In spite of everything—and in spite even of Miss Hatchard—Lawyer Royall ruled in North Dormer; and Charity ruled in Lawyer Royall's house. She had never put it to herself in those terms; bue she knew her power, knew what it was made of, and hated it. [*Summer*. Quoted by permission.]

Miss Hatchard represents tradition and has relatives in higher social spheres beyond North Dormer. The village library commemorates her great-uncle, and its mouldering state is symbolic. Lawyer Royall represents the modern world, though he no longer justifies the status in the village that he arrogates to himself. With his solemn pretensions and absurd observances, he is a caricature of a very small town public figure. Charity has been rescued by his late wife, but she owes her position to her successful resistance to seduction at an early age and her refusal of marriage; they are both grimly comic scenes—"This ain't your wife's room any longer. . . ."—"How long is it since you looked at yourself in the glass? . . . I guess you're not going to get your mending done for you that way twice." Pity for a "lonesome man" has become contempt. Her victory over him is complemented by her ability to shock Miss Hatchard by her basic knowledge of life. This, of course, does not establish her position in the village community which, as is usually the case toward outcasts, is hostile and derisive. The situation is changed by the arrival of Lucius Harney, who is making an architectural study of the old colonial houses that by their dilapidation help further to symbolize the state of the whole area. Charity's whole emotional and mental balance is disturbed, and out of this a love affair emerges, complicated by the intrigues of Royall, but as inevitable in the circumstances as Maggie Tulliver's love for Stephen Guest.

At this point Charity is brought back into contact with the Mountain people. Her attitude to her origin is very naturally ambivalent. She is ashamed of it before the village, but the bond of kinship nevertheless means something to her—and to them. She is brought into touch with one of the outlaws in a setting of great beauty to which she is responsive and he crudely not so. This in turn brings out the gap that separates her from them; the balancing up of attitudes becomes more and more interesting. She is as conscious of the gap between Harney and herself as between herself and the outlaws, and, when she realizes all he knows, "her whole soul [becomes] a tossing misery on which her hopes and dreams [spin] about like drowning straws." Her final attitude in his presence is represented by the simple assertion, "I ain't ashamed of them." Charity has now come to feel that "the sweetness of dependence" would be preferable to her "lonesome" dominion over Royall's bare and shabby house. It is her first normal human relationship. Harney could solve her whole problem of isolation, social as well as personal, by acting the part of the fairy prince and carrying her away into a new community; escape and social adjustment are dreamed of as identical. It is the waif's typical romantic vision. Harney, to revert to the comparison with *The Mill on the Floss,* is better class than Stephen Guest and is a young man of real culture, but he is a thoughtless philanderer who lives for the current moment. It would, however, be an exaggeration merely to call him a hypocrite. Nor should one apply the term without qualification to Royall, who is shown rather as a clear, and common, case of split personality; he is a windbag but he does not set himself up as a moralist. Charity next attempts contact with a much larger world. She deliberately involves herself in what might, if it were not superbly handled, read like the conventional story of the seduction of a village maiden. She insists on going to the town of Nettleton on the Fourth of July. The crowded, noisy, hot scenes in the train, in the trolley car, and on the lake steamer are all most vividly created; everything is seen through her eyes as new and glamorous. The climax, however, is a piece of sordid and ugly farce, which is doubly ironical, and the squalidly tragic background of Royall's tortuous behavior is made plain.

Charity's physical and emotional reaction is complete, and she is drawn back to the Mountain as the only community she belongs to. Old Home Week at North Dormer forms a brilliant—and ironical—serio-comic interlude, with Royall making just the right speech, representing the community values in public as completely as, in private for Charity, he represents sexual horror and the shame of her inferiority. But though her actual behavior may be regressive, her self-awareness, including ashamed bewilderment at her own behavior, shows how far she has developed in spirit. To complete her emotional education, she has after all, paradoxically to go back to her beginnings. Finding herself pregnant and knowing the village community's contempt for girls who married "to make things right," she sees only one possibility:

> Almost without conscious thought her decision had been reached; as her eyes had followed the circle of the hills her mind had also travelled the old round. She supposed it was something in her blood that made the Mountain the only answer to her questioning, the inevitable escape from all that hemmed her in and beset her. At any rate it began to loom in her again as it loomed against the rainy dawn; and the longer she looked at it the more clearly she understood that now at last she was really going there. [*Summer.* Quoted by permission.]

The climb up the Mountain through the first snow and her meeting with the parson who is going to bury her mother is very moving in its interplay of irony and pathos; it is another of those scenes where Edith Wharton avoids the sentimental risks with absolute assurance. One may mention that episcopal North Dormer does not seem to differ in moral atmosphere from sectarian Starkfield; a similar peasant hard-heartedness, varied with lapses into generosity, prevails. The funeral is one of Edith Wharton's great achievements:

> Mr. Miles paused and looked about him; then he turned to the young man who had met them at the door.
> "Is the body here?" he asked.
> The young man, instead of answering, turned his head toward the group. "Where's the candle? I tole yer to bring a candle," he said with sudden harshness to a girl who was lolling against the table. She did not answer, but another man got up and took from some corner a candle stuck into a bottle.
> "How'll I light it? The stove's out," the girl grumbled.
> Mr. Miles fumbled under his heavy wrappings and drew out a match-box. He held a match to the candle, and in a moment or two a faint circle of light fell on the pale aguish heads that started out of the shadow like the heads of nocturnal animals.
> "Mary's over there," some one said; and Mr. Miles, taking the bottle in his hand, passed behind the table. Charity followed him, and they stood before a mattress on the floor in a corner of the room. A woman lay on it, but she did not look like a dead woman; she seemed to have fallen across her squalid bed in a drunken sleep, and to have been left lying where she fell, in her ragged disordered clothes. One arm was flung above her head, one leg drawn up under a torn skirt that left the other bare to the knee: a swollen glistening leg witht a ragged stocking rolled down about the ankle. The woman lay on her back, her eyes staring up unblinkingly at the candle that trembled in Mr. Miles' hand.
> "She jus' dropped off," a woman said, over the shoulder of the others; and the young man added: "I jus' come in and found her."
> An elderly man with lank hair and a feeble grin pushed between them, "It was like this: I says to her on'y the night

before: 'If you don't take and quit'—I says to her. . . ."

Some one pulled him back and sent him reeling against
a bench along the wall, where he dropped down muttering
his unheeded narrative.

There was a silence; then the young woman who had been
lolling against the table suddenly parted the group, and stood
in front of Charity. She was healthier and robuster-looking
than the others, and her weather-beaten face had a certain
sullen beauty.

"Who's the girl? Who brought her here?" she said, fixing
her eyes mistrustfully on the young man who had rebuked
her for not having a candle ready.

Mr. Miles spoke. "I brought her! she is Mary Hyatt's
daughter."

"What? Her too?" the girl sneered. [*Summer.* Quoted by
permission.]

It is even more squalid and chaotic farce than the fair-
ground scene at Nettleton, a picture of Yahoos in the last
stage of decay, and the service itself, punctuated by imbecile bickering and drunken brawling, points the underlying tragic irony of the whole:

"I am the Resurrection and the Life," Mr. Miles began;
"he that believeth in me, though he were dead, yet shall he
live. . . . Though after my skin worms destroy this body, yet
in my flesh shall I see God. . . ."

In my flesh shall I see God! Charity thought of the gaping
mouth and stony eyes under the handkerchief, and of the
glistening leg over which she had drawn the stocking . . .

"We brought nothing into this world and it is certain we
can carry nothing out—"

There was a sudden muttering and scuffle at the back of
the group. "I brought the stove," burst out the elderly man
with lank hair, pushing his way between the others. "I wen'
down to Creston 'n' bought it . . . 'n' I got a right to take it
outer here . . . 'n' I'll lick any feller says I ain't. . . ."

"Sit down, damn you," shouted the tall youth who had
been drowsing on the bench against the wall.

"For man walketh in a vain shadow, and disquieteth
himself in vain: he heapeth up riches and cannot tell who
shall gather them. . . ."

"Well, it *are* his," a woman in the background interjected in a frightened whine.

The tall youth staggered to his feet. "If you don't hold your mouths I'll turn you all out o' here the whole lot of you," he cried with many oaths. "G'won, minister . . . don't let 'em faze you. . . ."

"Now is Christ risen . . ." [*Summer.* Quoted by permission.]

We have actually been shown the extremes of corruption and mortality; it is a far more impressive effect of contrast between prayer and its circumstances than Joe's repetition of the Lord's Prayer in *Bleak House*. Her flight from the encampment is as suggestively described as her ascent to it, and, at her meeting with Royall, the complete reversal of situation is indicated in a sentence:

Her first impulse was to crouch under the ledge till he had passed; but the instinct of concealment was overruled by the relief of feeling that someone was near her in the awful emptiness. She stood up and walked toward the buggy. [*Summer.* Quoted by permission.]

There has been a change on both sides. A new solicitude and humanity have been brought out in Royall, and Charity submits to his rough kindness and accepts the humble security and social respectability that he can offer. He marries her virtually without her consent, but on the wedding night he shows a quite unexpected delicacy. The ending is more complex than may appear at first sight. The exchange:

". . . You're a good girl Charity."

Their eyes met, and something rose in his that she had never seen there: a look that made her feel ashamed and yet secure.

"I guess you're good too," she said, shyly and quickly. [*Summer.* Quoted by permission.]

expresses on the surface mutual confidence and affection, but it cannot be taken as all's well that ends well, for it is based on a lie by Charity, while Royall is a grotesque old man and the permanence of his reformation can only be problematical. As far as they know it, they have each accepted the actuality of the other. As far as it goes, it is the kind of compromise that Edith Wharton thought was the essence of marriage and all satisfactory human relationships. Humdrum, not to say dreary, as Charity's new position in society is, it is a complex relationship after the simpler, if more romantic, loves and hates that have gone before, and therefore one might perhaps expect it to have a greater stability. Nevertheless, though Charity has been cured of her escapism and her atavism, the double disillusionment has been very painful and the solution of her problems carries within it further possibilities of disaster. Tragic and comic strands have been very closely interwoven in the whole story. However, the total imaginative vision of *Summer* has something of the concern with issues of suffering and evil that one associates with tragedies in the full sense.

5 Social Change and Moral Problems

I

Edith Wharton published *The Fruit of the Tree* in 1907, the same year as *Madame de Treymes,* and the contrast could hardly be greater; it shows her reaching out beyond even rural poverty in New England and urban poverty in New York and attempting to interpret the large-scale social and economic problems of contemporary America. *The Fruit of the Tree* was her contribution to "muckraking," the exposure in literature of the misery and corruption involved in the vast industrial expansion taking place in the Middle West. She joined forces with Dreiser, Norris, Upton Sinclair and the other realistic portrayers of the social turmoil. No one is going to claim for her the scope or the first-hand knowledge of these novelists; indeed she had to make some corrections in her background detail between the serial publication of the novel in *Scribner's Magazine* and the final version.[1] One must recognize, however, that in this phase of her brilliant early success she not only read the work of her very different contemporaries but she made this deliberate effort to deal with new material and unfamiliar experience.

The Fruit of the Tree is not a successful novel, considered in and for itself. The "muck-raking" theme is focused in the conflict of an enlightened individual with the industrial organization he works for, leading on to an

---

1. Blake Nevius has a note on this. See his *Edith Wharton,* p. 255.

Edith Wharton

unfortunate and unsuccessful marriage which in turn focuses the conflict more sharply. At this point a separate and personal moral problem is introduced, which is of such a kind as almost inevitably to outweigh everything else in the book. In the dénouement the two plots are blended together and there is some fine tragi-comic irony, but, though they both share a single broad theme, one is conscious of the dichotomy in the novel as a whole and of many peculiarities of emphasis.

The actual description and exposure of industrial conditions is concentrated in Book I. We are shown a big family textile mill in a squalid suburb of Hanaford, a town a day's journey from New York, and the principles on which it is managed are summed up in the comment, "It costs more to increase the floor space than maim an operative now and then"; furthermore, the medical services are not disinterested and the manager is corrupt as well as brutal. Out of this situation emerge the protagonists in the struggle, on the one hand John Amherst, the assistant manager, who has made himself as nearly as possible into a working man, and Justine Brent, a brilliant upper-class girl who is so unconventional for the time as to have become a nurse, and on the other hand the young widowed owner of the mill, Bessy Westmore, who is so conventional that it is said that at school she ought to have worn "a tag" to identify her, and her family and friends. Amherst is a remarkable and closely observed study and shows that, although Edith Wharton's knowledge of the industrial scene may have been limited, her knowledge of human types was of considerable width and depth. Amherst loves his work in industry and is a fighter for social justice who has no scruples about breaking through conventions. He has, as one might expect, no social graces and, like many men of his kind, he also lacks ordinary human understanding of almost every situation apart from the public and industrial. An intense individualist, he has little real feeling for other individuals and, though extremely self-centered, he does not really know himself. Justine Brent is a very different type of welfare-worker from Gerty Farish. We are not at once made aware of beauty but rather of lively intelligence and determination of character; later one thinks sometimes of a Lily Bart who has taken up a real professional career:

> He was aware that everything about her was quick and fine and supple, and that the muscles of character lay close to the surface of feeling; but the interpenetration of spirit and flesh that made her body seem like the bright projection of her mind left him unconscious of anything but the oneness of their thoughts. [Edith Wharton, *The Fruit of the Tree,* Charles Scribner's Sons, Bk. II, 17. Copyright 1907 Edith Wharton; renewal copyright 1934 William R. Tyler. Quoted by permission.]

Bessy Westmore, her father, and the family friend are introduced as visitors from another world, which in every sense they are. They merely stay in Hansford in an ornately conventional house—there is not even any ink in the ormolu-mounted inkwell—for as short a time as possible. The older generation are old New Yorkers and they serve as sophisticated commentators in elaborately witty, rather Jamesian dialogue. Mrs. Westmore is a figure out of the Trenor-Dorset world who lives for entertainment and sports—one sees a certain evolution in fashion here—but her appearance makes an immediate impact both on Amherst and on the reader:

> . . . Mrs. Westmore's beauty was like a blinding light abruptly turned on eyes subdued to obscurity. As he spoke, his glance passed from her face to her hair, and remained caught in its meshes. [*The Fruit of the Tree,* Bk. I, 3. Quoted by permission.]

In this way the relationship between Amherst and Justine Brent—which has been set going on a plane of moral idealism and philanthropy, joined with conspiracy against the established order—is superseded by a strongly emotional relationship, based in both cases, though in different ways, on novelty and inexperience. As things work out, it is Amherst who conducts the party round the mill and he is thus brought in contact with Bessy Westmore as the chief representative of the other side; the whole shocking situation, exemplified by a disastrous accident, makes a direct human impression on her, and despite the opposition of her business advisers, which culminates in Amherst's dismissal, a welfare scheme is set up. So far the main effect of the novel has depended on simple contrasts of squalor and misery with beauty and luxury, and of humanity, intelligence, and efficiency with complacency, injustice, and short-sightedness. The revolt has been abortive, but personal contacts have been made. It is worthy but not distinguished fiction of social protest.

Book II opens after a gap of three years with a truce between the reforming individuals and society. Justine is given steadily more and more importance, as the marriage of Amherst and Bessy becomes a more and more uneasy alliance. She has married him because of the fairly simple romantic attraction of his good looks and his unfamiliar background and personality; he, with his typical obtuseness and lack of human imagination, thought that she shared his philanthropy. The unhappy relationship is presented with remarkable objectivity and, after a preliminary victory for Amherst, it rapidly deteriorates. The life of Lynbrook, Bessy's home on Long Island, brings out to the full their incompatibility, and it is an odd result of her sympathetic nature that Justine is looked upon as a confidante by both sides. Amherst is returning more and more to the mill and Bessy is giving herself up to social gaiety and sport—she rides a horse called Impulse; even her child Cicely "likes Justine best." As Amherst and Bessy reach a personal crisis, financial crisis also impends on both the social and the socialistic worlds. There is a fine scene of mistaken inferences that ends with Bessy's superbly, but of course quite unintentionally, ironic complaint that he has broken into her habit of church-going.

Edith Wharton opens the next phase with the virtually direct comment "that compromise is the law of married life," which, taken in many ways according to the mood of particular books, seems to be the simple maxim underlying all her studies of marriage, and which in this glaring case of self-ignorant and warring egotisms is specially apposite. The next truce, based on axed philanthropy and limited entertaining is more precarious—Lynbrook is as oppressive to Amherst as Westmore Mills to Bessy. There is a strain of actual evil in the book, but the Lynbrook world breaks up as a result of its own internal tensions; Amherst escapes to the mill again and Bessy brings back her most frivolous friend. The victory of Society does not last long, as Bessy not only follows her impulses but rides the horse and is thrown and injures her spine. The conflict now becomes not merely complex but confused. Justine rises to new heights of disinterested devotion to the friend she had once actively despised, and from this follows the mercy-killing. Edmund Wilson is right in this case; the episode is an artistic blunder.[2] It is true that it can be taken as a supreme and fatal act of individual social enlightenment and personal devotion, but it is almost inevitably melodramatized and overweighted with all the passions of the time and it sets going a sequence of sin, repentance, and expiation movements, derived in their turn from Puritan traditions, which, interesting though some of the psychological repercussions are in themselves, blurs and distorts the development of the earlier conflict.

Given the euthanasia, the events of Book IV have their own logic. Amherst and Cicely have inherited the mills and he proceeds with his schemes, confident that despite

2. *The Wound and the Bow*, p. 199.

everything Bessy approved them; the picture of innocent egotism is complete. The scene of his proposal to Justine is good ironic comedy, especially, if we remember his previous marriage, her final remark:

> "I'm just like other women you know. I shall like it because it's your work." [*The Fruit of the Tree*, Bk. IV, 31.]

In the event they "compromise" in a full sense, but the revelation of the crime brings about a fantastic distortion of the whole situation. The scenes are crowded one on top of another and the writing is often inflated. Nevertheless, the outwardly happy ending is, in effect, bitterly ironic tragedy. Amherst and Justine have reached a further "compromise" in ceaseless expiatory good works and they have secured the approval of society both as a whole and with a capital "S." But in a deeper sense Society has won. Amherst is so obsessed by guilt that he believes in a completely false image of Bessy as a kind of goddess of philanthropy, and he deceives himself into treating her last extravagant scheme for Lynbrook as a design for a recreational center for Hanaford, while Justine's "full price" in humiliation is tacitly to accept this lie. Amherst seems to have convinced himself that he has transformed the actuality of Hanaford and the mill into something quite near the ideal, but this appearance of achievement and of devotion to each other and to their work on the part of himself and Justine covers a ghastly degradation of spirit and confusion of motives. They are doing the right deeds for both the wrong and the right reasons at the same time. There is considerable power of emotion suggested in this last Book even though it is not always fully expressed on the page, but the almost macabre intensity of the guilt obsession weighs down the later course of the conflict and indeed infuses a painful and almost tragic bitterness, where an ending in enhanced self-knowledge for Amherst and ironically comic compromise, which drew the two sides together without any pretense of obliterating their differences, might have been possible.

II

The short stories that Mrs. Wharton collected in her volumes, *The Hermit and the Wild Woman*, 1908, *Tales of Men and Ghosts*, 1910, and *Xingu*, 1916 include some distinguished work. The title story of the first belongs with her other medievalizing sketches to a period fashion and the supernatural stories also are not very interesting contributions to a genre. On the other hand, the stories that dramatize, without adventitious aids, a psychological condition or a problem of moral choice have kept their interest even though particular situations may belong in some cases to out-of-date social custom. Here one appreciates the subtlety and delicacy of the handling and the fineness of the values involved. One or two stories may be said to achieve a genuine artistic autonomy.

The Verdict and *The Pot-Boiler* are both concerned with the artistic conscience. One is reminded of James's stories of novelists, though Edith Wharton's stories are much slighter work. Like James's writers, Mrs. Wharton's artists inhabit the edges of the fashionable world. *The Pot-Boiler* presents an elaborate, though formalized situation. We have a painter who is a real artist and a very "sincere" but mediocre sculptor, both unsuccessful financially. In changed circumstances the sister of the sculptor berates her brother's friend for sacrificing his convictions, but goes on ". . . you must see the distinction because you first made it clear to me. I can take money earned in good faith—I can let Caspar live on it. I can marry Mr. Mungold because, though his pictures are bad, he does not prostitute his art." One infers that the mere fashionable artist who paints as well as he is able does not deserve censure and that, though one may prostitute oneself for the sake of art, art is sacred. It is a clear moral and aesthetic judgment.

Edith Wharton's artist-heroes compel actuality to identify itself with the ideal whatever the human cost. Her stories of other problems are less ruthless in their upshot and more leisurely and deeper in treatment. Irony is pervasive in all of them, accentuating pathos and the tragic in the marriage and divorce stories but absurdity and the comic in the treatment of most other themes. *His Father's Son* and *The Blond Beast* deal with parental relationships. From the point of view of the characters they may be said to be based on conflict between the ideal and actuality— Mason Grew in the first talks about "the big view" and Orlando G. Spence in the second talks of "principle." Looked at from the outside by the reader through the author's eyes, the idealism seems more a matter of keeping up appearances; as social and moral criticism the comedy works in that way, but below this there is a layer of sympathetic psychological analysis. *His Father's Son* is a picture of absurd romanticism and vicarious living. Mason Grew is shown as living on his son's social success, which is a ridiculous situation, but the value of the story lies in the way we see the dependence of both characters on their illusions and, in the case of the father, see that he sees this too. The combination of sympathy and criticism that is Edith Wharton's final attitude is implied in Mason Grew's words on the last page,

"Look at here, Ronald Grew—do you want me to tell you how you're feeling at this minute? Just a mite let down, after all, at the idea that you ain't the romantic figure you'd got to think yourself . . . Well, that's natural enough, too; but I'll tell you what it proves. It proves you're my son right enough, if any more proof was needed. For it's just the kind of fool nonsense I used to feel at your age—and if there's anybody here to laugh at it's myself, and not you. And you can laugh at me just as much as you like." [Edith Wharton, which by its simple forthrightness exposes both of them, but leaves us with a general sense of human frailty rather than foolishness.

The Blond Beast has a similar quality. It is brilliant satire and the central scene in which the millionaire philanthropist dictates his sentiments during luncheon and condoles with his secretary for missing the soufflé is one of Edith Wharton's funniest pieces of dramatization. The millionaire is a comparatively simple study of humbug—"it was one of Millner's discoveries that an extremely parsimonious use of the emotions underlay Mr. Spence's expansive manner and fraternal phraseology . . ." Draper Spence, his son, reflects his father's philanthropy on another plane by holding Bible classes in a poor district, but Millner, the secretary, is more complex. The story is told as it is registered by his consciousness; in his developing attitude lies the full effect. Millner begins by feeling that:

> The opportunity of a clever young man with a cool head and no prejudices (this again was drawn from life) lay rather in making himself indispensable to one of the beneficent rich, and in using the timidities and conformities of his patron as the means of his own advancement. Young Millner felt no scruples about formulating these principles to himself. It was not for nothing that, in his college days, he had hunted the hypothetical "moral sense" to its lair, and dragged from their concealment the various self-advancing sentiments dissembled under it. His strength lay in his precocious insight into the springs of action, and in his refusal to classify them according to the accepted moral and social sanctions. He had to the full the courage of his lack of convictions. ["The Blond Beast," in *Tales of Men and Ghosts.* Reprinted by permission.]

His critical detachment is gradually weakened until a

complete reversal of situation is brought about; Millner discovers in himself impulses that he had not previously acknowledged and he sees the need for even Spence's vast structure of hollow idealism as a source for his son's very existence. Once again, underlying the satire of the whole and the absurdity of the details, there is the feeling for the interdependence of human needs and qualities.

The stories of matrimonial problems form a distinct group. It would be idle to deny that the subject had a special personal interest for Mrs. Wharton, though there is nothing unduly personal in the matter or the manner. They are poised and ironical like the rest, but there is a stronger feeling of pathos and even tragedy. It would be fair to say that, in terms of what James called "felt life," these stories merit the most attention of the work in this form up to date. *The Letters* is a curious and a noteworthy production, especially as it was written before *The Reef.* It is extraordinarily disillusioned and yet completely un-embittered. Edith Wharton makes the worst of her chosen situation and yet makes happiness grow out of it. A governess, who inherits a fortune, is married in peculiarly unpropitious circumstances by a former employer and made aware of descending degrees of casualness until the bottom is reached when, three years later, she finds all her pre-marital letters to him—unopened. The ending clearly implies the author's comment:

> As her husband advanced up the path she had a sudden vision of their three years together. Those years were her whole life; everything before them had been colourless and unconscious, like the blind life of the plant before it reaches the surface of the soil. The years had not been exactly what she had dreamed; but if they had taken away certain illusions they had left richer realities in their stead. She understood now that she had gradually adjusted herself to the new image of her husband as he was, as he would always be. He was not the hero of her dreams, but he was the man she loved, and who had loved her. For she saw now, in this last wide flash

of pity and initiation, that, as a comely marble may be made out of worthless scraps of mortar, glass, and pebbles, so out of mean mixed substances may be fashioned a love that will bear the stress of life. ["The Letters," in *Tales of Men and Ghosts*. Quoted by permission.]

One almost feels that Edith Wharton is teaching a lesson in the meaning of mutual toleration and acceptance of the plain reality of ourselves, but once again it is all dramatized for us vividly to experience it. It is an individual relationship, not a mere type case. Sadness and absurdity are just about equally balanced.

The Long Run is near tragedy in that the hero fails, because he is what he is, to accept the great opportunity of his life when it comes to him. The story is distanced a little by the use of double narration, but this makes possible a preliminary sketch of the background in old New York with "exceedingly 'nice' " "unobtrusive" people and portraits of Merrick, the brilliant young man who has become "conventional and rather dull," and Paulina, the faded beauty and her rich, commonplace second husband. The rest of the story is a subtle self-portrait, in part ironical, in part directly self-critical, of a fundamentally timid man who resembles several of Edith Wharton's other old New-Yorkers and also suggests a male version of Anna Leath. Out of Merrick's own mouth we hear an account of his "robust passion" for Paulina during her first marriage, of her offer to give up everything for love and how he had prevaricated with all the arguments of conventional prudence. It is a most powerful scene and the mode of telling makes it devastating to the narrator, Merrick himself, however inevitable may be its conclusion; "life-as-it-is, in contrast to life-as-a-visiting-list" is what he has never faced except intellectually. The ending is tragic-comic; "the long run" shows that the risks would have been worth taking. Whereas the heroine of *The Letters* makes the best of an actuality that the author has begun by making the worst of, it is, in this case, the hero who deliberately makes the worst of life.

Autres Temps takes a long-term view of divorce in the social context of New York Society before the First World War. The title is ironical and the effect depends once again on balance, this time of two juxtaposed situations. The whole treatment is subtler and more restrained than in *The Long Run,* but nevertheless full of poignancy. On one plane it is a comedy of manners in the full sense, on another a pathetic personal tragedy. The two situations are those of a mother, Mrs. Lidcote, who left her husband long ago and had to go away and is used to being "cut," and her daughter, Leila, who has also divorced her husband and remarried. The gist of the story is that it is *"autres moeurs"* for Leila but not for her mother. After some quietly ominous scenes in New York, the full implications emerge at a country house party where Mrs. Lidcote is in fact kept out of her daughter's life by a mixture of guile, apparent solicitude for her fatigue, and, above all, her *own* tact:

> "Then won't they think it odd if I don't appear? . . . Will they think it odd if I *do*?" ["Autres Temps," in *Xingu and Other Stories.* Quoted by permission.]

By such typically conversational understatements, Leila's time-serving and her mother's moral triumph but social defeat are conveyed to us. It is a further irony that Leila and her mother really are fond of each other; probably only within the conventions of the time could this mutual affection have survived.

These stories are the product of mature and studied art and of a well-balanced and intelligent attitude to Society and its conventions; one could cite a number of observations such as: "Traditions that have lost their meaning are the hardest of all to destroy." Mrs. Wharton contemplates her problems in their individual and social implications. Her irony of so many kinds, from the straight satirical to the almost tragic, forms a continuous indication of her sense of complexity. She offers no final solutions but, in showing her characters' solutions, she makes us conscious of certain simple values of sincerity and understanding.

III

Xingu, the title story of the 1916 volume, deals with the permanent rather than the changing in Society and the subject is a state of affairs rather than a problem. The material is the American cultural association; it had been the Uplift Club in *The Legend* and is the Lunch Club in *Xingu.* In both these cases she uses it as the basis for satiric comedy of pretentious social appearances and discrepant reality. *Xingu* is an American *Précieuses Ridicules,* and its distinction as a story lies in the all-inclusive demolition of affectation that is contrived. The mode is farcical.

The ladies of Hillbridge claim "to centralize and focus its intellectual effort," and each is a beautifully sketched individual portrait of social and the most superficial kind of intellectual snobbery. The opening scene just suggests that Mrs. Roby may really be more cultivated than the others, who illustrate various forms of empty pretence, but one soon finds that she represents mere honest frivolousness combined with a certain quickness of wit. The central episode, in which Osric Dane, a celebrated woman novelist, is entertained, is brief and brilliant farce, from the scene in the drawing-room, with copies of books on which the members feel they ought to be "up" scattered on the table, to the crucial "discussion." In this Mrs. Roby is made to show up everyone, the pompously superior novelist and the fatuous pursuers of culture. She slips in the title word as their current interest and an earnest conversation is constructed as if they all knew what it meant:

> "It has done me worlds of good," Mrs. Leveret interjected, seeming to herself to remember that she had either taken it or read it the winter before.
>
> "Of course," Mrs. Roby admitted, "the difficulty is that one must give up so much time to it. It's very long."
>
> "I can't imagine," Miss Van Vluyck, "grudging the time given to such a subject."
>
> "And deep in places," Mrs. Roby pursued; (so then it was a book!) "And it isn't easy to skip."
>
> "I never skip," said Mrs. Plinth dogmatically.
>
> "Ah, it's dangerous to, in Xingu. Even at the start there are places where one can't. One must just wade through."
>
> "I should hardly call it *wading*," said Mrs. Ballinger sarcastically.
>
> Mrs. Roby sent her a look of interest. "Ah—you always found it went swimmingly?"
>
> Mrs. Ballinger hesitated. "Of course there are difficult passages," she conceded.
>
> "Yes; some are not at all clear—even," Mrs. Roby added, "if one is familiar with the original."
>
> "As I suppose you are?" Osric Dane interposed, suddenly fixing her with a look of challenge.
>
> Mrs. Roby met it by a deprecating gesture. "Oh, it's really not difficult up to a certain point; though some of the branches are very little known, and it's almost impossible to get at the source." ["Xingu," in *Xingu and Other Stories.* Quoted by permission.]

The absurdity rises to a climax as each asserts that it is something quite different and deflation is completed by the discovery that it is a river in Brazil and that everything Mrs. Roby has said could, as one can see, be applied to a river, as neatly and expressively as Sir John Denham once hoped that his description of the Thames could be applied to his poetry.[3] Nothing has been left

3. Though deep, yet clear, though gentle, yet not dull,
   Strong without rage, without o'erflowing, full.
                              Cooper's Hill, 1643 (text of 1668)

standing except this lady's honesty and mischief. Edith Wharton has avoided the obvious contrast of introducing a genuinely cultivated person and in this way given her satire more devastating implications. But it is as a *jeu d'esprit* that one values *Xingu;* it is both highly intelligent and very funny.

6 Comedy in Society

Henry James wrote two pages in praise of *The Custom of the Country* that provide an invaluable basis for discussion of the book's qualities. He sees in it both concentrated richness of detail and sustained effect of tone.

We have it from her not in the crude state but in the extract, the extract that makes all the difference for our sense of an artistic economy. If the extract, as would appear, is the result of an artistic economy . . . we find it associated in Mrs. Wharton with such appeals to our interest, for instance, as the fact that, absolutely sole among our students of this form, she suffers, she even encourages, her expression to flower into some sharp image or figure of her thought when that will make the thought more finely touch us. Her step, without straying, encounters the living analogy, which she gathers, in passing, without awkwardness of pause, and which the page then carries on its breast as a trophy plucked by a happy adventurous dash, a token of spirit and temper as well as a proof of vision. . . . Mrs. Wharton's reaction in presence of the aspects of life hitherto, it would seem, mainly exposed to her is for the most part the ironic. . . . *The Custom of the Country* is at any rate consistently, almost scientifically satiric as indeed the satiric light was doubtless the only one in which the elements engaged could at all be focussed together. But this happens directly to the profit of something that, as we read, becomes more and more one with the principle of authority at work; the light that gathers is a dry light, of great intensity, and the effect, if not rather the very essence, of its dryness is a particular fine asperity. . . . We move in an air purged at a stroke of the old sentimental and romantic values . . . and we shall not here attempt to state what this makes for in the way of esthetic refreshment and relief. . . .

114

A shade of asperity may be in such fashion a security against waste, and in the dearth of displayed securities we should welcome it on that ground alone. It helps at any rate to constitute for the talent manifest in *The Custom* a rare identity, so far should we have to go to seek another instance of the dry, or call it perhaps even the hard, intellectual touch in the soft, or call it perhaps even the humid, temperamental air; in other words of the masculine conclusion tending so to crown the feminine observation.[1]

It is indeed magnificent comedy. Fine as *The House of Mirth* is, one can, though one may not share them, appreciate doubts as to Lily Bart's adequacy as a vehicle of tragic experience. One has no such doubts about Undine Spragg as a comic figure. She seems at times a kind of female Tamburlaine[2] in her combination of lust for conquest and love of splendor, but in the full context one sees her rather as a great Jonsonian figure who in the end meets her match. The mode of the book is that kind of vigorous comic caricature, and the construction, with its brilliantly visualized episodes, has obvious resemblances to drama. Everything fits together; Edith Wharton's "realistic" social criticism is the kind that depends on consistent stylization of character and dialogue. The formally harmonious but concrete, and often, as James points out, wittily and vividly figurative prose may be illustrated by two studies of minor characters:

> The Princess, who might have been of any age between twenty and forty, had a small triangular face with caressing impudent eyes, a smile like a silent whistle and the gait of a baker's boy balancing his basket. She wore either baggy shabby clothes like a man's, or rich draperies that looked as if they had been rained on; and she seemed equally at ease

1. "The New Novel," reprinted in *The Art of Fiction*, ed. Roberts, New York: Oxford University Press, 1948, pp. 209–10.

2. I was of course thinking of the character in the play. I was interested to notice that Louis Auchincloss at about the same time, thought of the historical Genghis Khan, *op. cit.*, p. 105.

in either style of dress, and carelessly unconscious of both. She was extremely familiar and unblushingly inquisitive, but she never gave Undine the time to ask her any questions or the opportunity to venture on any freedom with her. Nevertheless she did not scruple to talk of her sentimental experiences, and seemed surprised, and rather disappointed, that Undine had so few to relate in return. She playfully accused her beautiful new friend of being *cachottiére,* and at the sight of Undine's blush cried out: "Ah, you funny Americans! Why do you all behave as if love were a secret infirmity?"

The old Duchess was even more impressive, because she fitted better into Undine's preconceived picture of the Faubourg Saint Germain, and was more like the people with whom she pictured the former Nettie Wincher as living in privileged intimacy. The Duchess was, indeed, more amiable and accessible than Undine's conception of a Duchess, and displayed a curiousity as great as her daughter's, and much more puerile, concerning her new friend's history and habits. But through her mild prattle, and in spite of her limited perceptions, Undine felt in her the same clear impenetrable barrier that she ran against occasionally in the Princess; and she was beginning to understand that this barrier represented a number of things about which she herself had yet to learn. She would not have known about this a few years earlier, nor would she have seen in the Duchess anything but the ruin of an ugly woman, dressed in clothes that Mrs. Spragg wouldn't have touched. The Duchess certainly looked like a ruin; but Undine now saw that she looked like the ruin of a castle. [Edith Wharton, *The Custom of the Country,* Charles Scribner's Sons, Bk. III, 27. Copyright 1913 Edith Wharton; renewal copyright 1941 William R. Tyler. Quoted by permission.]

The dry but imaginative humor of her observation in cases such as these forms a basis for the greater asperity or indignation that inspires the creation of more important personages. A very elaborate structure of social ideals is built up and subjected to detached and impartial scrutiny, and the manners and customs of each group are displayed and their moral quality exposed as Undine Spragg sweeps forward from one to another. The central theme is her pursuit of wealth and power, cutting across the conflicts of groups and classes, old and new. The positive values are diffused. It is not merely a matter of old New York against the newly rich or European tradition against trans-Atlantic innovation. There are humane and civilized qualities and simple truth and generosity in many places, often the most unexpected. They emerge from the social struggle as it progresses and form an implicit judgment on the final ironic victory.

The opening scenes have indeed the air of being distilled extracts from overflowing experience and the descriptions focus for us with almost the force of metaphor the peculiar life that the heroine and her parents have inflicted on themselves. Whereas Lily Bart begins with a subordinate but recognized place in Society, Undine Spragg does not know at the beginning what Society even looks like. She and her parents have come to New York from Apex in the Middle West—one thinks of Sinclair Lewis's Zenith—as one family in a band of what can only be called modern nomads, who have no idea of how to live in their new circumstances of affluence. Except for the husbands when they are in their offices downtown, they are more lost and out of place than Charity Royall in North Dormer. Edith Wharton presents this extraordinary social phenomenon of the unabsorbed newly rich with a mixture of mockery of the milieu and sympathy for its more innocent dupes. There are foretastes in *The House of Mirth,* but here we get the full picture of the rich of several vintages. The Spraggs carry on an absolutely rootless and utterly boring existence amid the comfortless, tasteless, and depersonalized luxury of a "Looey suite" in the Hotel Stentorian, a name happily chosen to indicate the tone of its more prominent inhabitants. Mrs. Spragg wears "as complete an air of detachment as if she had been a wax figure in a shop-window." Her one interest is the daughter's social advancement. Mr. Spragg, on the other hand, despite his drooping and dyspeptic appearance, has not altogether lost his "pioneering" energy. There is a certain Dickensian quality about their presentation in terms of typical and

slightly absurd details of dress and behavior. The artificiality of the two women's existence is epitomized in the
decidedly Dickensian character of Mrs. Heeny, the mas-
seuse and manicurist, who provides them and others like
them with a vicarious social life as well as physical invig-
oration. Her advice, "Go steady, Undine, and you'll get
anywheres," is recalled at intervals during the heroine's
progress. As has been indicated, Undine Spragg begins her
career of conquest from the outside. She has to be shown
not only the territory and the membership of Society but
also its scale of values, the difference between Washington
Square and Fifth Avenue, the difference between the
Dagonets and Marvells, on the one hand, and the Driscolls
and Van Degens, on the other, and which is the more
"swell"—plain white or pigeon-blood note paper. She is
at once a formidable and an absurd figure. She is beautiful
in a rather blatant way, with reddish-gold hair and dark
eyebrows, and from childhood she has had a narcissistic
strain that has become an ingredient in a naïve but predatory egotism:

> Already Undine's chief delight was to "dress up" in her
> mother's Sunday skirt and "play lady" before the wardrobe
> mirror. The taste had outlasted childhood, and she still prac-
> tised the same secret pantomime, gliding in, settling her skirts,
> swaying her fan, moving her lips in soundless talk and
> laughter; but lately she had shrunk from everything that
> reminded her of her baffled social yearnings. Now, however,
> she could yield without afterthought to the joy of dramatizing
> her beauty. Within a few days she would be enacting the scene
> she was now mimicking; and it amused her to see in advance
> just what impression she would produce on Mrs. Fairford's
> guests.
>   For a while she carried on her chat with an imaginary
> circle of admirers, twisting this way and that, fanning, fidget-
> ing, twitching at her draperies, as she did in real life when
> people were noticing her. Her incessant movements were not
> the result of shyness: she thought it the correct thing to be
> animated in society, and noise and restlessness were her only

notion of vivacity. She therefore watched herself approvingly, admiring the light on her hair, the flash of teeth between her smiling lips, the pure shadows of her throat and shoulders as she passed from one attitude to another. [*The Custom of the Country*, Bk. I, 1. Quoted by permission.]

There is a hint of the tigress here, mingled with the naivety. She tyrannizes over her parents by sheer petulance and she soon adapts her posturings to the task of subduing other worthwhile victims. She is described as "fiercely independent and yet passionately imitative" so that, while always seeking to dominate, she picks up the manners of whatever group she is placed in. Her most terrifying and far-reaching quality is her coldness. She has tremendous energy but no human sympathy, let alone passion. With one exception, her relationships with men are motivated by social ambition, sometimes of a ridiculously childish kind, and she casts them off if she is not socially satisfied. Where Lily Bart is shown as frivolous, but ultimately pathetic, Undine Spragg is ruthlessly calculating. One cannot call her contemptible, however; she rises—it is the appropriate word—to wickedness on a majestic scale in her indifference to moral principles and her freedom from the ties of affection; relative chastity is a mere byproduct of her frigidity. She has none of the charm and warm-heartedness of Becky Sharp, to whom she has been compared; no one would ever try to sentimentalize Undine Spragg. One thinks rather of a more respectable and more successful, but less human, Roxana; Edith Wharton's ironical detachment is indeed comparable to the coarser quality in Defoe. With all her meretricious glamor and her dominant position, Undine is a perfectly adjusted component in the satiro-comic scheme. If it can be called Undine *contra mundum*, both sides and all parts stand or fall together as art as certainly as one side stands or falls as life.

Book One works by a series of strongly contrasted ironic juxtapositions. It is an ironical accident that Undine's first real social contact is with the inner stronghold of old New York Society, as its manners especially are beyond her comprehension. A dinner party, the simplicity of which disappoints her, shows up her vulgarity of speech and illiteracy of interests—she has no conversation and the only novel she has read is called *When the Kissing Had to Stop*—but on the other hand her "violent longing to brush away the cobwebs" reflects an ironic attitude on the author's part toward Washington Square. The conservative refinement and the deliberate avoidance of ostentation suggest a certain lack of vitality in Ralph Marvell's family. By way of contrast Undine is brought into contact with the millionaire Fifth Avenue world, already, of course, linked by marriage to Washington Square—Mrs. Peter Van Degen is Ralph Marvell's cousin. There is a hint of attraction toward the hideous "saurian" figure of Peter Van Degen but it is the world of luxury he represents, not the man, that draws her sympathy; this kind of life is the consummation of all her adolescent dreams and she can understand it at sight. An opera box puts her briefly in contact with both worlds at once, that of the philistines who patronize the arts for prestige alone and that of the cultivated. Her deepening feeling for Ralph Marvell—it is a mixture of real attraction to his good looks and pride in her own power—and his feeling for her are placed against a background of social comparisons made by Ralph himself, which in fact begin to reveal for us the underlying attitude of the book. Ralph Marvell is disgusted by the new Society, especially when it makes gestures of cultivation and artistic patronage, which are traded on by the fashionable portrait painter, Popple, the type of the charlatanry and sycophancy that such a community always breeds, and we see him reverting to earlier loyalties:

> Ralph sometimes called his mother and grandfather the Aborigines, and likened them to those vanishing denizens of

the American continent doomed to rapid extinction with the advance of the invading race. He was fond of describing Washington Square as the "Reservation", and of prophesying that before long its inhabitants would be exhibited at ethnological shows, pathetically engaged in the exercise of their primitive industries.

Small, cautious, middle-class, had been the ideals of aboriginal New York; but it suddenly struck the young man that they were singularly coherent and respectable as contrasted with the chaos of indiscriminate appetites which made up its modern tendencies. He too had wanted to be "modern", had revolted, half-humorously, against the restrictons and exclusions of the old code; and it must have been by one of the ironic reversions of heredity that, at this precise point, he began to see what there was to be said on the other side—*his* side, as he now felt it to be. [*The Custom of the Country*, Bk. I, 5. Quoted by permission.]

His meditations, however, carry him on to reflect again on the cultivated but "desultory dabbling" that represents life for him and for his kind. He thinks of their "archaic probity that had not yet learned to distinguish between private and 'business' Honour," but he realizes that "the daughters of his own race [are selling] themselves to the Invaders; the daughters of the Invaders [are buying] their husbands as they [buy] an opera-box." He becomes more and more conscious of the mingling of the old and new upper classes; they all speak "the same language." At this point his perceptiveness becomes blurred by romanticism, and the critical placing of him also becomes apparent. Ralph Marvell appreciates the simplicity and frankness of the Spraggs, the fact that they have "been 'plain people' and [have] not yet learned to be ashamed of it," but when he begins to build up a vision of an alliance between these "primitives" and the Dagonets and to see himself as Undine's savior from Van Degenism, the absurdity of his delusions is clear and the final vision, by its mock-heroic reference, clinches the matter:

He seemed to see her—as he sat there, pressing his fists into his temples—he seemed to see her like a lovely rock-bound Andromeda with the devouring monster Society careering up to make a mouthful of her; and himself whirling down on his winged horse—just Pegasus turned Rosinante for the nonce—to cut her bonds, snatch up her, and whirl her back into the blue. [*The Custom of the Country*, Bk. I, 6. Quoted by permission.]

The gist of it would seem to be that the values of old New York are morally and culturally superior to those of the newly rich, though capable of equivocation, but they are not only incapable of survival in any struggle for existence —we know Edith Wharton had read Darwin—but also mediocre and cramping for finer spirits such as Marvell, let alone the more energetic. Ralph Marvell has more energy than Lawrence Selden, but less detachment and psychological penetration. He is ready to act, but also easily deceived, so that with all his intellectual flexibility and vitality, which raise him above his own group, he is still, partly because of his cloistered upbringing and partly because of his retired and introvert temperament, pre-destined to be a victim of Undine. She provides many opportunities for his romantic idealization. It is in this way that attitudes are built up and criticized as we go and that Edith Wharton's discriminations are manifest. Chapter VI is a key chapter. Its relationship to the social, economic, and cultural diagnoses in *A Backward Glance* are obvious and once again one is dazzled by the clarity of Edith Wharton's vision so early in her career as a writer. Nor is her social criticism ever mere commentary. The battle of "Invaders" and "Aborigines" is always fully realized drama; the critical judgments are enacted in satiric creation.

The engagement dinner is an occasion for some fine multiple irony. It is Undine's first great social victory, but her vulgar and frivolous talk of divorce is both ominous in itself and gives old Mr. Dagonet the opportunity to score at least a conversational point, "My child, if you look like that you'll get everything," which again carries layers of meaning in terms of the superior manners of old New York and, echoing Mrs. Heeny, in terms of prophecy of her future. The rest of the Book is occupied with revival of the past and preparation for long-term development. Elmer Moffatt, the young man with whom Undine has been connected at Apex, is reintroduced. He is now a hanger-on of millionaire business and a maneuver on his part that is very close to blackmail shows how precarious the whole order of new and old New York can be. He represents the power of sheer business enterprise, another and yet less scrupulous and more iconoclastic generation undermining both the millionaires of Fifth Avenue and the new arrivals in the hotels, not to mention Washington Square. He is merely sketched but very suggestively sketched, at this stage:

> Nevertheless something in his look seemed to promise the capacity to develop into any character he might care to assume; though it did not seem probable that, for the present, that of a gentleman would be among them. [*The Custom of the Country*, Bk. I, 9. Quoted by permission.]

He is made at one moment cheaply arch—"Where's your chaperon, Miss Spragg? . . . Allow me to escort you to the bewfay," and at another crudely forthright "I mean *you* to talk. . . . It's a hundred thousand down, between us." Edith Wharton here begins the creation of yet another type, one whose development is to run parallel with that of Undine until the final reunion. He is made marvelously common in every word and every detail of dress and gesture.

Book Two presents the course and breakdown of Undine's marriage to Ralph Marvell and the end of her association with old New York. The honeymoon in Italy reveals to each their absolute incompatibility of tastes and temperament. In the face of European civilization she retains her simple-minded vulgarity and her barbarian extravagance. Her egotism is becoming more heartless and rises from exasperation, when her father loses money, to hysterical fury at the inconvenience of pregnancy and callous neglect of her son when he is born. Hers is an active and aggressive egotism where that of Rosamond Vincy, with whose character and situation also she has something in common, is passive and parasitic. She is moving steadily into the Van Degen group, simply because its pleasures seem natural to her:

> She felt the strength of Van Degen's contempt for everything he did not understand or could not buy: that was the only kind of "exclusiveness" that impressed her. And he was still to her, as in her inexperienced days, the master of the mundane science she had once imagined that Ralph Marvell possessed. During the three years since her marriage she had learned to make distinctions unknown to her girlish categories. She had found out that she had given herself to the exclusive and the dowdy when the future belonged to the showy and the promiscuous; that she was in the case of those who have cast in their lot with a fallen cause, or—to use an analogy more within her range—who have hired an opera box on the wrong night. It was all confusing and exasperating. Apex ideals had been based on the myth of "old families" ruling New York from a throne of Revolutionary tradition, with the new millionaires paying them feudal allegiance. But experience had long since proved the delusiveness of the simile. Mrs. Marvell's classification of the world into the visited and the unvisited was as obsolete as a mediaeval cosmogony. [*The Custom of the Country*, Bk. II, 14. Quoted by permission.]

The choric character, Charles Bowen, attributes the estrangement of Undine from Ralph to the conditions of American life:

> "Where does the real life of most American men lie? In some woman's drawing-room or in their offices? The answer's

obvious, isn't it? The emotional centre of gravity's not the
same in the two hemispheres. In the effete societies it's love,
in our new one it's business. . . . Isn't that the key to our
easy divorces? If we cared for women in the ofd barbarous
possessive way, do you suppose we'd give them up as readily
as we do?" [*The Custom of the Country*, Bk. II, 15. Quoted
by permission.]

But, though this represents the general drift of the book
and its relationship to the general social situation of the
time, the case of Ralph and Undine is even more special
than Bowen makes it. Ralph is not interested in business
and he is simply not a match for her impulse to dominate.
His disillusionment is indicated by a series of significant
episodes, beginning with the discovery that she has had
his family jewels reset and lied about the fact, which makes
clear to him her utter indifference to all he believes in.
However, his opinion that she will not risk "bother" of any
kind is confirmed in an amusing scene with Van Degen:
"already in her short experience she [has] seen enough
of the women who sacrifice future security for immediate
success, and she [means] to lay solid foundations before
she [begins] to build up the light superstructure of enjoyment." It is pathetically ironical that Ralph Marvell's
vision of common ground between the Spraggs and his
family only materializes when Undine blandly talks to her
father about divorce; however "elastic" his business morality, the idea of a woman's wanting to leave her husband
merely because she is bored is "as shocking to him as it
would have been to the most uncompromising of the
Dagonets and Marvells." However, the reintroduction of
Moffatt makes a compromise possible. This time he puts
Ralph in the way of making money and thus makes it
possible for Undine to go back to Europe; he has previously paid for her wedding in a similar way! These
interventions by Moffatt in the role of *deus ex machina*
may seem indeed somewhat mechanical coincidences but

within the "well-made" technique of the novel they have considerable significance. Moffatt has close associations with Undine and, with what Ralph Marvell calls his "epic effrontery," his pursuit of power is complementary to hers. We are beginning to visualize *his* ruthless and unscrupulous vigor. We also see at this point, within the hard-boiled manner, a certain engaging humanity in his attitude to the unfortunate little Paul Marvell, which is not paralleled in Undine.

The scenes that follow display Undine's idea of happiness, subtly focused in the ironical vision of the commentator, Charles Bowen:

> During some forty years' perpetual exercise of his perceptions he had never come across anything that gave them the special titillation produced by the sight of the dinner-hour at the Nouveau Luxe: the same sense of putting his hand on human nature's passion for the factitious, its incorrigible habit of imitating the imitation. [*The Custom of the Country*, Bk. II, 19. Quoted by permission.]

Through his eyes also we get an elegant idealized portrait of a new character, representing the introduction of a whole new theme:

> Raymond de Chelles, who came of a family of moderate fortune, lived for the greater part of the year on his father's estates in Burgundy; but he came up every spring to the *entresol* of the old Marquis's hotel for a two months' study of human nature, applying to the pursuit the discriminating taste and transient ardour that give the finest bloom to pleasure. Bowen liked him as a companion and admired him as a charming specimen of the Frenchman of his class, embodying in his lean, and fatigued and finished person that happy mean of simplicity and intelligence of which no other race has found the secret. If Raymond de Chelles had been English he would have been a mere fox-hunting animal, with appetites but without tastes; but in his lighter Gallic clay the wholesome territorial savour, the inherited passion for sport and agriculture, were blent with an openness to finer

sensations, a sense of the come-and-go of ideas, under which one felt the tight hold of two or three inherited notions, religious, political, and domestic, in total contradiction to his surface attitude. That the inherited notions would in the end prevail, everything in his appearance declared, from the distinguished slant of his nose to the narrow forehead under his thinning hair; he was the kind of man who would inevitably "revert" when he married. [*The Custom of the Country*, Bk. II, 19. Quoted by permission.]

Undine herself is conscious of the resemblance between Chelles and Ralph Marvell, between the representative French nobleman and the representative upper-class old New Yorker—only Mrs. Heeny calls the Marvells aristocrats—and she is attracted in an ominously similar way. She makes use of him at this point, however, to bring about—inadvertently—the great blunder of her career, a display, at the very moment of her surrender to Peter Van Degen, of the sheer beastliness to which her egotism can descend.

The episode with Peter Van Degen and its aftermath bring out into full view an aspect of Undine that has previously been only adumbrated, and also certain fundamental differences of moral outlook between the groups and classes involved. It has been seen that the Marvells and the Spraggs disapprove of divorce, though in the one case the disapproval is absolute, with the whole Puritan tradition behind it; in the other it is qualified by the more relaxed belief that a woman is entitled to get rid of a guilty partner with as little unpleasantness as possible and to avoid further unpleasantness. The attitude of Undine is more utilitarian, but nevertheless strictly respectable, and she is embarrassed by the assumption of emancipation that her present situation gives rise to in the easy-going cosmopolitan company she frequents:

The pleasures for which her sex took such risks had never attracted her, and she did not even crave the excitement of having it thought that they did. She wanted passionately and persistently, two things which she believed should subsist together in any well-ordered life: amusement and respectability; and despite her surface-sophistication her notion of amusement was hardly less innocent than when she had hung on the plumber's fence with Indiana Frusk. [*The Custom of the Country,* Bk. III, 24. Quoted by permission.]

We are shown her in company with the said Indiana and similar characters to whom "respectability is the breath of life." They share a certain crassness of speech that differs from both Peter Van Degen's more upper-class and slangy vulgarity and Elmer Moffatt's lower-class glibness of wit; they are indifferent to, and even frequently shocked by, art and literature. Undine has got a long way on this basis. She has escaped from the dreary and bewildered vacancy of her parents' existence, and she has tried and found old New York beyond her intellectual powers and cramping to her ideals of fashion and gaiety. She has failed with the millionaires whose way of life, apart from their adoption of aristocratic ideas of sexual morality, is the only one that suits her. She is thus ready for the conquest of a new world of pleasure and social glory and her previous contact with the French aristocracy provides the obvious opportunity. The next section of the pattern is decidedly complicated. As she did with those of old New York, Undine has made herself conversant with the traditions and outward customs of the class without appreciating, still less understanding, them. We are shown, on the one hand, her approaches to Chelles and his family, which are so wary as to serve as coquetry, and, on the other hand, a renewed encounter with Moffatt that stirs "the fibres of a self she [has] forgotten but [has] not ceased to understand"; the suggestion of revived physical passion is blended with the suggestion of two adventurers reunited. The upshot is a project, arising from a combination of Undine's not exactly simulated, but decidedly equivocal, maternal affection, and—ironically—Moffatt's liking for the child, to use her rights of full custody as a means of forcing enough money out of the Marvells to cover the expense of the annulment that would be necessary for her to remarry into a Catholic noble family. There is of course a further layer of meaning deriving from Moffatt's admiration for Undine and willingness to help her on all occasions and a further layer still deriving from his sheer lack of scruples and contempt for old New York. Undine's reluctance to entertain the suggestion is one of her redeeming moments, her succumbing to it is her most immoral action, deliberately and wantonly cruel and doubly deceitful.

Book Four shows the impact of her action on Ralph Marvell. Against a background of characteristic Marvell fussing over scandal, he turns to Moffatt for financial help. The simple irony of the situation as regards Moffatt's part in it does not need emphasis, but the juxtaposition of values and modes of action is extreme. Ralph Marvell at his most helpless and sensitive is confronted with a man who does not pretend even to the veneer of gentlemanliness that the Invaders have acquired from the Aborigines. An unnecessary remark provokes a natural reaction:

> "I wouldn't have alluded to it now if you hadn't taken rather a high tone with me about our little venture; but now it's out I guess you may as well hear the whole story." [*The Custom of the Country*, Bk. IV, 35. Quoted by permission.]

When Moffatt goes on to reveal his own early marriage to, and divorce from, Undine, he seems to Ralph Marvell the very personification of vulgarity, but the interpretation of Ralph's feelings about himself and Moffatt's last words suggests more than a record of the working out of historical necessity:

> He seemed to be stumbling about in his inherited prejudices

like a modern man in mediaeval armour . . . Moffatt still sat at his desk, unmoved and apparently uncomprehending. "He doesn't even know what I'm feeling," flashed through Ralph; and the whole archaic structure of his rites and sanctions tumbled down about him.

Through the noise of the crash he heard Moffatt's voice going on without perceptible change of tone: "About that other matter now . . . you can't feel any meaner about it than I do, I can tell you that . . . but all we've got to do is to sit tight." [*The Custom of the Country*, Bk. IV, 35. Quoted by permission.]

Moffatt, representing the latest wave of new wealth, is several stages more "elastic" in his principles, both private and public, than Mr. Spragg; he is an amoral human animal, a genial barbarian, without delicacy or scruple but without malice. Ralph is pathetic, but his romanticism, with all its background mixture of Puritan morality and unsophisticated middle-class chivalry, cannot engage one's full sympathy. Old New York cannot cope with the facts of life and instead makes futile gestures of defiance or revulsion. Ralph has regressed more and more into it; his last gesture is as quixotic as his earliest vision of marriage and as ridiculous as that vision has proved itself to be. He has disintegrated as a character; his early intellectual impulses toward revaluation of traditions and relaxation of conventions and his early desire for a more independent life have long ago lost momentum, but nevertheless we recognize his good qualities and pity him as the victim of circumstance, and we also have to recognize that he and his family represent the finest as well as the narrowest and silliest qualities of old New York. What is valuable there remains in suspense in the mind for the final reckoning.

Book Five of *The Custom of the Country* is a *tour de force* of construction in the full sense that it presents a triumphant final development of themes and a comic catastrophe, commensurate with the scale of the novel. Undine's egotism reaches its apogee in terms of social success, and the ironic nature of her last achievement conveys, after the satiric demolition of so much else, her final comic exposure. Henry James's verbal criticism that Edith Wharton ought to have made the whole novel out of the French confrontation misses the point of the sequence that leads up to it and the conclusion that follows, even more completely that she herself says.[3] One thinks again of the Jonsonian analogy. When it comes to the end, one does not, however, have quite the familiar spectacle of two rogues, double-crossing each other until both go under together, but instead one has a new alliance of two megalomaniacs whose values and manners will never quite coincide with or complement each other. The Book opens with Undine in scenes of aristocratic dignity in the Faubourg St. Germain but in conditions, if not of noble poverty, at least of confinement to an *entresol* flat in the Hotel de Chelles and under the constant surveillance of her husband:

> Raymond seemed to attach more importance to love, in all its manifestations, than was usual or convenient in a husband; and she gradually began to be aware that her domination over him involved a corresponding loss of independence. [*The Custom of the Country*, Bk. V, 37. Quoted by permission.]

The irony of the situation is intensified by the next scene, which shows Undine, now a Marquise, amid the mouldering splendor, material austerity, and hidebound etiquette of the ancestral Château de Saint Désert; the detail is superbly chosen and some of it has a nightmare quality:

> Undine, through the slow hot crape-smelling months, lived encircled by shrouded images of woe in which the only live points were the eyes constantly fixed on her least movements. [*The Custom of the Country*, Bk. V, 38. Quoted by permission.]

---

3. *A Backward Glance*, p. 182.

Edith Wharton builds up the French aristocratic community with a skill equal to that shown in describing old New
York or the more sprawling world of the millionaires. The
idealized first impression of Raymond de Chelles is replaced by a portrait of a man of real strength of character,
practical ability, worldly wisdom, and deep intelligence,
standing out from, but fully belonging to, a class and a
way of life whose manners, moral principles, and economic
organization, whatever the incidental corruptions, make
old New York look the narrow-minded and upstart little
place it was:

> To *faire valoir* the family acres had always, it appeared,
> been Raymond's deepest-seated purpose, and all his frivol-
> ities dropped from him with the prospect of putting his hand
> to the plough. He was not, indeed, inhuman enough to con-
> demn his wife to perpetual exile. He meant, he assured her,
> that she should have her annual spring visit to Paris—but he
> stared in dismay at her suggestion that they should take pos-
> session of the coveted *premier* of the Hotel de Chelles. He was
> gallant enough to express the wish that it were in his power
> to house her on such a scale; but he could not conceal his
> surprise that she had ever seriously expected it. She was be-
> ginning to see that he felt her constitutional inability to un-
> derstand anything about money as the deepest difference be-
> tween them. It was a proficiency no one had ever expected her
> to acquire, and the lack of which she had even been encour-
> aged to regard as a grace and to use as pretext. During the
> interval between her divorce and her remarriage she had
> learned what things cost, but not how to do without them;
> and money still seemed to her like some mysterious and un-
> certain stream which occasionally vanished underground but
> was sure to bubble up again at one's feet. Now, however, she
> found herself in a world where it represented not the means
> of individual gratification but the substance binding together
> whole groups of interests, and where the uses to which it
> might be put in twenty years were considered before the
> reasons for spending it on the spot. At first she was sure she
> could laugh Raymond out of his prudence or coax him round
> to her point of view. She did not understand how a man so
> romantically in love could be so unpersuadable on certain

points. Hitherto she had had to contend with personal moods, now she was arguing against a policy; and she was gradually to learn that it was as natural to Raymond de Chelles to adore her and resist her as it had been to Ralph Marvell to adore her and let her have her way. [*The Custom of the Country,* Bk. V, 38. Quoted by permission.]

Edith Wharton holds up Chelles and his way of life for our respectful admiration, but there is no simple-minded and awe-stricken endorsement of the new values. All of it, including his excessively black suits and his lumbering brougham and the compromises necessitated by the indiscretions of his younger brother, is presented with the same detachment. The gradual estrangement between Undine and her new husband is developed in terms comparable to her previous marital breakdown, with the great difference that Raymond de Chelles can withdraw gradually into a self-contained, active, and cultivated world of his own; Ralph has no such self-sufficiency, though both he and old New York are, allowing for all the limitations, presented more sympathetically than aristocratic France. We are made more and more aware of contrasts between absurd discomfort and inherited magnificence on the one hand and childishly narcissistic extravagance on the other, until the vividly revealing scene when Undine suggests selling the château:

The colour came slowly to his face, but it hardened into lines she had never seen. He looked at her as though the place where she stood were empty. "You don't understand," he said again. [*The Custom of the Country,* Bk. V, 40. Quoted by permission.]

followed later by his denunciation of everything she stands for:

"And you're all alike," he exclaimed, "every one of you. You come among us from a country we don't know, and can't imagine, a country you care for so little that before you've

been a day in ours you've forgotten the very house you
were born in—if it wasn't torn down before you knew it! You
come among us speaking our language and not knowing what
we mean; wanting the things we want, and not knowing why
we want them; aping our weaknesses, exaggerating our fol-
lies, ignoring or ridiculing all we care about—you come from
hotels as big as towns, and from towns as flimsy as paper,
where the streets haven't had time to be named, and the
buildings are demolished before they're dry, and the people
are as proud of changing as we are of holding to what we
have—and we're fools enough to imagine that because you
copy our ways and pick up our slang you understand anything about the things that make life decent and honourable
for us!" [*The Custom of the Country*, Bk. V, 42. Quoted by
permission.]

The negative side of this diatribe expresses the implicit
attitude of the book in an extreme way, appropriate to the
context, and contrasts with Ralph Marvell's pained and
mute acceptances; the Chelles's positives are less irre-
proachable, and it is worth noting that we are never made
to see through Raymond de Chelles's eyes. Despite the
respect invited of, and—surely—felt by, the reader, we are
not made aware of him as a human presence to the same
extent as with Ralph Marvell. Both are, however, values,
and they should be regarded as complimentary.

The magnitude of Undine's social success and her unsuitability to enjoy it are now equally apparent. Whatever
the limitations and the hypocrisies of the French aristocratic world, it is plain that, just as in the case of old New
York, she lacks the cultural equipment to fit into it. By a
brilliant manipulation of associated ideas she is made
suddenly to realize that Elmer Moffatt could give her all
the material splendor that Chelles can give and a gay social life as well. There is something mock-heroic in her
new vision, especially when she thinks back to a scene of
hilarious and shameless farce at the Temperance Society
at Apex. The scene that precedes Undine's elopement with

Moffatt is a wonderful laying bare of realities and exchange of simple sincerities. His attitude to Undine is quizzical—"You're not the beauty you were . . . ," and he cuts through all her acquired aristocratic subterfuges to the direct statement:

> "Look here, Undine, if I'm to have you again I don't want to have you that way. That time out in Apex, when everybody in the place was against me, and I was down and out, you stood up to them and stuck by me. Remember that walk down Main Street? Don't I . . . and if you want to come back you've got to come that way: not slink through the back way when there's no one watching, but walk in by the front door, with your head up, and your Main Street look." [*The Custom of the Country*, Bk. V, 45. Quoted by permission.]

Chelles has been stronger than Undine, but Moffatt really beats her at her own game of power. He emerges as a most remarkable creation; he combines vulgarity and virility, business ruthlessness and social horse sense, a simple solidity that Peter Van Degen lacks and a primitive *panache* that is lacking in Chelles. He insists on a reunion on plain Middle West "boy meets girl" terms. The final chapter provides the ironic commentary. The Moffatt *hôtel* in Paris surpasses all previous visions of splendor—he has even managed to buy the Chelles tapestries, and Undine, by a delightful touch, has pigeon-blood rubies. It seems the product of the imagination of a respectable Sir Epicure Mammon. But, parodying it all, the absurd Mrs. Heeny is still in attendance, and wandering ill at ease is young Paul Marvell. He is a much finer creation than Cicely, the poor little rich girl of *The Fruit of the Tree,* and he carries his significance as tragic victim and residuary legatee of both old New York and traditional France with no traces of sentimentality or awkwardness. His fruitless search for his own possessions, his desire to get at the locked-up books, and his unsatisfied curiosity about the

pictures are perfectly in the character of a serious small
boy and at the same time symbolize the natural civilized
human being isolated amid completely artificial conditions. He not unnaturally, and from the point of view of
the themes very appropriately, blurs the memory of Ralph
Marvell with that of his French "father," whom he has
loved, and he is outraged by Moffatt's crassness and his
mother's lies about the latter. He is made to enact the
fundamental criticism of Undine and Moffatt that under-
lies the whole story of their careers in all its significance,
the cold cruelty of Undine's egotism and Moffatt's coarse-
grained obtuseness. Paul Marvell's tears are deeply
poignant. The last note is satiric comedy. Undine has not
lost her social ambitions and she has acquired considerable
social expertise, but her own past and Moffatt's vulgarity
will always queer her pitch, and Moffatt has got *her* for
his wife. They now belong to no class, and they have no
traditions and no principles, inherited or acquired; they
have only each other and unlimited wealth. The comic
prospect is endless and unrelieved.

It is, as James says, "the masculine conclusion," a supremely intelligent balancing up of accepted customs and
the potentialities of the time. Edith Wharton was not to
return to the theme of social conflict until after the First
World War had shaken all the old customs and let loose
most of the potentialities.

7 *Old New York*

Although Walter Berry prophesied that nobody else except themselves would be interested in the New York of her childhood, *The Age of Innocence,* 1920, was serialized in *The Pictorial Review* and was, almost inevitably, awarded the Pulitzer Prize and has become one of Edith Wharton's most widely read and admired works. It has all the ingredients of a historical best-seller, a richly detailed period setting, an emotional situation that the modern reader can flatter himself, or more important, herself would work out more happily at the present day and, combined with the appeal to critical superiority, a pervasive nostalgia for the past. It is, with all its faults, manifestly the product of a distinguished creative·mind, if in a consciously relaxed mood, and it does not suffer from the wholly untypical rawness and nerviness of feeling, the uncertainty of tone and attitude that characterize *A Son at the Front,* which was being planned at the same time. The Puritanical element in the New York tradition comes out in *The Age of Innocence* much more strongly than in any part of *The Custom of the Country* and, remembering that Edith Wharton there uses the name Marvell, one is reminded in this later novel of *A Definition of Love.* There is, of course, no ground for supposing that she consciously took her theme from that poem, but the relationship between Newland Archer and Ellen Olenska has an air of being

> . . . begotten by Despair
> Upon Impossibility.

137

Everything in the situation is against them, the whole weight of a social and moral tradition. Nevertheless, as with the situation in *The Reef,* one finds it pathetic—and sometimes absurd—rather than tragic, and the elaborate moral solution and the epilogue rather heavily sentimental. The social conflict, of the individual against the group, is comparable to that of Lily Bart with a later New York Society, but it is muted and muffled by the mass of period upholstery. It is not merely that the age enthroned "Taste," that far-off divinity of whom "Form" was the mere visible representative and vicegerent; the whole story on both sides is especially fully visualized in terms of clothes and interior decoration, and documented with accounts of manners, customs, and social history. As in the case of the fully historical *Valley of Decision,* Edith Wharton is, to put it simply, more concerned to recreate a past age than to say something she thinks important about life. There is a lack of emotional pressure and ironic tension; elegant as the writing undoubtedly is, it lacks the hard precision of the best earlier books. After all, the stimulus to such writing was not there in the chosen subject matter, except on one or two occasions.

The New York world is re-created in full and fascinating detail. This is the genuine old New York of the 70s, before the millionaires of *The House of Mirth* had built their mansions on Fifth Avenue. We are given illustrative examples to those early paragraphs in *A Backward Glance.* Book One brings before us the moral and emotional situation in relation to that wealthy but in every way thoroughly provincial and middle-class community, which is perhaps most strikingly and fantastically epitomized by the fact that women imported dresses in the latest fashion from Worth and then kept them for two years before wearing them. The pattern of this little "Society" had come to seem part of the order of nature, incredible as this may seem:

New York, as far back as the mind of man could travel, had been divided into the two great fundamental groups of the Mingotts and Mansons and all their clan, who cared about eating and clothes and money, and the Archer-Newland-van-der-Luyden tribe, who were devoted to travel, horticulture and the best fiction, and looked down on the grosser forms of pleasure. [Edith Wharton, *The Age of Innocence*, Charles Scribner's Sons, Bk. I, 5. Copyright 1928 Edith Wharton; renewed copyright 1955 William R. Tyler. Quoted by permission.]

Edith Wharton's use of the words "clan" and "tribe" is deliberate and recurring. The people who actually wrote books and painted pictures did not belong to either group. They did not want to, and Society was never sure whether they were really "ladies" and "gentlemen." One moves on to note the finer distinction between the van der Luydens and two other families of aristocratic origin and the rest and, complicating the situation, the independent positions of old Mrs. Manson Mingott, a comic figure of monstrous obesity, and of Julius Beaufort, the rich financier, who is blatantly vulgar and openly disreputable. Two characters have a kind of choric function as representatives of the social spirit: they are Lawrence Lefferts who

. . . was, on the whole, the foremost authority on "form" in New York. He had probably devoted more time than anyone else to the study of this intricate and fascinating question; but study alone could not account for his complete and easy competence. One had only to look at him, from the slant of his bald forehead and the curve of his beautiful fair moustache to the long patent-leather feet at the other end of his lean and elegant person, to feel that the knowledge of "form" must be congenital in anyone who knew how to wear such good clothes so carelessly and carry such height with so much lounging grace. [*The Age of Innocence*, Bk. I, 1. Quoted by permission.]

and old Mr. Sillerton Jackson, the authority on "family":

He knew all the ramifications of New York's cousinships, and could not only elucidate such complicated questions as that of the connection between the Mingotts (through the Thorleys) with the Dallases of South Carolina, and that of the relationship of the elder branch of Philadelphia Thorleys to the Albany Chiverses (on no account to be confused with the Manson Chiverses of University Place), but could also enumerate the leading characteristics of each family. [*The Age of Innocence*, Bk. I, 1. Quoted by permission.]

It was an inflexible social pattern and it is very suitable that we should get our first panorama of it as Newland Archer, the hero, surveys the audience at the opera, an institution where all the traditional European social rituals were assiduously imitated. Ellen Olenska is conspicuous because her dress, though elegant, is not quite conventional. The Archer family, although belonging to the more intellectual section of Society, are shown as weighed down with conventional habits, and the implications of Newland Archer's gestures of rebellion are not always fully understood even by himself; sometimes he sees his marriage "with a shiver of foreboding becoming what most of the other marriages about him [are]: a dull association of material and social interests held together by ignorance on the one side and hypocrisy on the other." But he is "sincerely but placidly in love" with the "frankness" and "freshness," based of course on utter ignorance, of his bride, May Welland, and looks forward to guiding her vague cultural gestures. One can see that they are in fact predestined to become a typical New York couple, if of slightly wider interests than the majority. Newland Archer is too gentlemanly, too committed to the regime of doing the right things, of avoiding unpleasantness of all kinds and, especially, of ignoring the loose living of many of his associates. Presumably, in order to make life viable at all for a relatively small, wealthy, and leisured community, the moral atmosphere had been allowed to settle down in this way; only dishonesty in business or flagrant sexual irregularity was condemned. Yvors Winters sums up *The Age of Innocence* by saying that it illustrates an ethical tradition more ancient than Calvinist Puritanism, though modified by it:

> . . . the characters are living in a society cognate and coterminous with those principles; the society with its customs and usages, is the external form of the principles. Now the customs and usages may become unduly externalized, and when they appear so to become, Mrs. Wharton satirizes them; but in the main they represent the concrete aspect of the abstract principles of behavior.[1]

He goes on to discuss the relationship of Archer and Ellen Olenska in terms of their having to abandon a way of life that they in fact find satisfying and admirable, if they decide to rebel openly against its moral principles. This indicates the situation in the long run.

In the short run everything possible is done to absorb the Countess Olenska into Society and neutralize her possibly disturbing influence. Even the aristocratic van der Luydens are moved to lend her their prestige. Ellen Olenska, though a cousin, is a foreign and, at least potentially, a revolutionary force. She settles in a street between the purlieus of Society and Bohemia, has unusual decorations and unwittingly compromises herself by entertaining doubtful company—old New York snobbery did not extend to an English duke for his rank alone. The charm of Ellen Olenska is made very real. She is beautiful, smart, intelligent, original in her taste, generous and guileless; she is not a mere "made-over" version of the Baroness Munster, though the general idea of the book is, of course, related to that of *The Europeans*. The contrast between her and May Welland is brought out again when May goes so far as to cut church to walk with Archer in the Park, but causes him to say:

---

1. *Maule's Curse* reprinted in *In Defense of Reason*, London: Routledge, 1960, p. 309.

"Original! We're all as like each other as those dolls cut
out of the same folded paper. We're like patterns stencilled
on a wall. Can't you and I strike out for ourselves, May?"
[*The Age of Innocence*, Bk. I, 10. Quoted by permission.]

But Archer's subjection to convention comes out in his
advice to Ellen to avoid a divorce with its risks of scandal
and one reaches the point at which he has let his engagement to May go forward because he is not quite sure of
Ellen's innocence and Ellen feels, "I can't love you unless
I give you up"; in other words, she feels that she must
accept the conventions of New York because its narrow-
minded community has after all made her feel happy and,
paradoxically, even free. Fate has crowded itself betwixt
them in the double guise of social convention, with its
whole lineage of moral principle, and of family solidarity
and generosity which, if they take effect a little slowly and
grudgingly, nevertheless manifest themselves in very solid
and material forms. The worst and best of old New York
are inseparable. Everyone is too "nice" for the heights and
depths of passion to have scope. The mere humbugs and
the absurder customs are satirized, but in the rest of the
picture Edith Wharton is resurrecting the historical types
and evoking the scenes she remembered without her customary play of irony. The central situation is presented
in all solemnity without seeming tragic; from Edith Wharton one would have expected something analogous to the
wit of Marvell's poem.

Newland Archer's two relationships now develop rapidly. The fashionable wedding is described with much
detail of dress and behavior, and, after this, his disappointing honeymoon in Europe, which shows up May as scarcely
more cultivated than Undine Spragg is shown to be in
similar circumstances, followed by a Newport season with
all its archaic ritual. It is therefore inevitable that Archer
should drift back toward Ellen. A curious relationship is
established depending on

... the perfect balance she had held between their loyalty to others and their honesty to themselves that had so stirred and yet tranquillized him; a balance not artfully calculated, as her tears and her falterings showed, but resulting naturally from her unabashed sincerity. It filled him with a tender awe, now the danger was over, and made him thank the fates that no personal vanity, no sense of playing a part before sophisticated witnesses, had tempted him to tempt her. [*The Age of Innocence*, Bk. II, 25. Quoted by permission.]

This relationship, with all the magnanimity it implies—it is a kind of "magnanimous despair" leading to a love of "divine" ideality—is offered for our unqualified admiration. May's conventionality and unsuitability as a wife for Archer are made painfully obvious; his throwing open a window on a cold evening symbolizes his feeling of claustration. Ellen's moral superiority to everyone around her becomes equally obvious in her demonstrative kindness to Mrs. Beaufort after the bank failure—old New York's human worst side was plainer than its commercial best on such occasions. Her clear-sightedness sees the frequent dinginess of the lives of unmarried couples where Archer has only his own sort of conventional romantic visions. But the alternative she offers of love in separation—"in reach and yet out of reach" or, at the most, "Shall I—once come to you; and then go home?"—lacks, for all the gratitude and generosity towards the feelings of her friends underlying it, a certain fundamental humanity. It is not in the context tantalizing and coy, as might appear in quotation, but very idealized. Her fineness has some of the rarefied quality of Anna Leath's, though none of the meanness, and she certainly does not suffer from Lily Bart's vein of frivolousness. Despite her past experience, she will not or cannot face the consequences of a break with social conventions. As Winters says,[2] a formal social order, with all its restrictions, seems to her to provide a more satisfactory

---

2. *Ibid.*

way of life than freedom in isolation. The situation is wound up with the most meticulous regard for old New York conventions. Ellen Olenska has decided to return to Europe—we learn afterwards that May has precipitated this by a piece of deceit; the Archers give the farewell dinner, and the hypocrisy is an occasion for some magnificent satiric conclusions in Edith Wharton's most trenchant manner—here the writing really comes to life:

> There were certain things that had to be done, and if done at all, done handsomely and thoroughly; and one of these, in the old New York code, was the tribal rally around a kinswoman about to be eliminated from the tribe. There was nothing on earth that the Wellands and Mingotts would not have done to proclaim their unalterable affection for the Countess Olenska now that her passage for Europe was engaged.
>
> It was the old New York way of talking life "without effusion of blood"; the way of people who dreaded scandal more than disease, who placed decency above courage, and who considered that nothing was more ill-bred than "scenes," except the behaviour of those who gave rise to them. [*The Age of Innocence*, Bk. II, 33. Quoted by permission.]

Archer is made conscious of all the irony and the suspicions and of his helplessness in the grip of the genteel tradition, and we are shown a bitterly satiric picture of the victory of the two petty tyrants of Form and Family.

Nevertheless, the final solution can only be taken as a sentimental endorsement of the tribal code. Archer settles down as a model husband—he and May "compromise" by ignoring awkward realities to the end. In the epilogue he reemerges as a public-spirited citizen who has worked with Theodore Roosevelt, but he refuses the chance of a reunion with Ellen when it comes thirty years later. Though Archer has become a more active representative of old New York than Selden or Marvell, one is asked to reverence the persistence of tradition rather than admire its flexibility. The possible pointer toward the later chapters of *The Buccaneers* is not sufficiently followed up to make it truly significant. Edith Wharton apparently endorses both old New York and Ellen Olenska's and Archer's renunciation of each other, which indeed, in its idealism, also belongs to old New York; Ellen Olenska is not completely foreign after all. This is a rather sugary version of the kind of conflict that leads to Lily Bart's tragedy. To compare it with the brilliantly comic interplay of values and foibles that James creates in *The Europeans,* where the Baroness after doing so much to aerate the atmosphere of New England lets herself down with a fib, is to realize how leisurely and lacking in vitality *The Age of Innocence* is as a whole. One cannot help also realizing, however, that in its nostalgic escapism, which she admits to in *A Backward Glance,* it is also personal to the author in other ways. One recalls, in connection with Ellen Olenska's attitude, Mrs. Wharton's exclamation quoted by Percy Lubbock, "Ah, the poverty, the miserable poverty, of any love that lies outside of marriage, of any love that is not a living together, a sharing of all!"[3] These words, dating from about 1912, the year of her separation, and about two years after the end of her affair with Morton Fullerton, might have been spoken in the novel and one feels that, in creating Ellen Olenska and giving her human vitality and definition in a world of wax works, Edith Wharton may have been projecting an idealized vision of herself into the Society of her youth, where one knows she was in fact a rather colorless participant. Now that we know how far Mrs. Wharton in fact differed from Ellen Olenska, we see both the pathos and the irony of such an idealization. Anna Leath and, later, Rose Sellars are comparable, though older, types of elegant austerity; but they are more austere and also much

---

3. *Portrait of Edith Wharton,* p. 100

more critically presented. Edith Wharton is surely in all three, partly idealizing and partly criticizing, in various combinations, her own complex nature, her refined puritanism, inherited and temperamental, and her sometimes concealed, sometimes repressed, capacity for human warmth and passion. It would be impertinent to speculate any further until more documentary evidence is available, but one also feels that the identification is supported by her creation of comparable types of elegant austerity in Anna Leath and, later, Rose Sellars. It is difficult to say how far this represents a vein of Puritan tradition and how far a temperamental compulsion, insofar as these could in any case be separated.

In the *Old New York* stories, 1922 to 1924, Edith Wharton goes back into reported history, beginning with the forties; their chief interest is social. *False Dawn* demonstrates how very middle class indeed the manners of the top layer of New York Society had been within the lifetime of Edith Wharton's older contemporaries, and *New Year's Day* gives us a very seamy picture of the age of innocence; Edith Wharton presents a situation of considerable pathos and implies a further and even more damning criticism of the pettier conventions of the time. The series brings to an end Mrs. Wharton's concern with the uneasy position of the individual in a closely integrated and exclusive social group where ordered and polished appearances are the expression of moral ideals and principles and the divergencies of errant reality may be not only ridiculous but also shocking.

8 Satire on Society

I

Edith Wharton's association with *The Pictorial Review* might well seem to lead to an artistic, if commercially successful, dotage. *Glimpses of the Moon*, 1922, is a careless and ill-written first study of the socially anarchic twenties, with a young American couple, who in fact resemble in a sentimental way Lily Bart and Lawrence Selden, trying to make a life for themselves with a minimum of help from traditional forms and sanctions. It is a comedy of inconsistencies, which the two protagonists end by achieving a measure of maturity. *The Mother's Recompense*, 1925, is more serious in intention and presents a moral "problem." The "shocking" problem and the compromise solution are carefully draped, to avoid giving offense while at the same time inviting the magazine public "to think." Though the question of whether incest—the word is mentioned once—should in the special circumstances of the novel be condoned is a particular moral issue rather than a representative social tension, it might have had a tragic seriousness against a complete old New York puritanical background. But the chief concern now is the avoidance of suffering by the diffusion of coziness and the assiduous concealment of anything thought to be nasty. Opportunities for irony are constantly being lost in the sentimental haze that surrounds Kate Clephane, who has been invited back from a little community of similar *déracinés* on the Riviera—a mildly satiric picture—to live with her long-deserted daughter on Fifth Avenue. The central problem, the daughter's prospective marriage, is twofold: the mother knows the man is thoroughly unreliable, and she has also slept with him. Kate Clephane is shown as a very ordinary, not to say rather silly, individual, who is trying to cope with what she *feels*, rather than *thinks*, is evil. The reader today feels that, worthless as the man may be, it is not possible in the context of decaying principles and confused impulses fully to sympathize with her horror of the marriage as an "unnatural" relationship.

But as Edith Wharton's understanding of the 1920s became deeper and more comprehensive and as her attitude toward it crystallized, she found the right mode for her interpretation of it, namely rough satire. Satire is, of course, a pervasive ingredient in her earlier work, especially *The Custom of the Country,* but in *Twilight Sleep* and *The Children* the life of the rich is treated with consistent contempt, and values are represented by isolated individuals and small groups who are shown struggling, not against a tyrannous code, but against anarchy in morals and manners—what Richard Chase calls "the mannered lack of manners" of the time. Nona Manford in *Twilight Sleep* says, "I know most of the new ways of being rotten; I only wish I was sure I knew the best way of being decent. . . ." The Van Degens and the Moffatts and their children are now Society and the old attitude to them is very naturally transferred to the mass; it is a mass rather than a group. Surviving old New Yorkers are now isolated individuals also, rather than representatives of a traditional hierarchy, and one finds them allied to the well-intentioned and bewildered young. The loss of traditional social standards and the need to rely on personal choice are indeed sometimes felt as a disadvantage by characters who actually play a

leading part in the new world. Emancipation all the time
is shown to be a condition with which very few can cope;
despite the elasticity of her conscience, Mrs. Manford is
relieved that her corsets prevent her sitting on the floor.

II

In *Twilight Sleep*, 1927, Edith Wharton lets herself go
as a literary artist in the Fifth Avenue world of the Jazz
Age. Every detail vividly objectifies the predominant mood
and the situation develops with an exhilarating momentum. If the novel appears less closely constructed than the
best earlier work, this is because Edith Wharton is not
plotting the graph of one character's career, but deploying
a group of people in circumstances that are bound to ex-
pose their weaknesses. The portrait of a minor character
may again be used to illustrate the mode of a great part
of the book:

"11.45 Mrs. Swoffer."
  Oh, to be sure . . . Mrs. Swoffer. Maisie had reminded her
that morning. The relief was instantaneous. Only, who *was*
Mrs. Swoffer? Was she the President of the Militant Pacifists'
League, or the Heroes' Day delegate, or the exponent of the
New Religion of Hope, or the woman who had discovered a
wonderful trick for taking the wrinkles out of the corners
of your eyes? Maisie was out on an urgent commission, and
could not be consulted; but whatever Mrs. Swoffer's errand
was, her arrival would be welcome—especially if she came
before her hour. And she did.
  She was a small plump woman of indefinite age, with
faded blond hair and rambling features held together by a
pair of urgent eye-glasses. She asked if she might hold
Pauline's hand just a moment while she looked at her and
reverenced her—and Pauline, on learning that this was the
result of reading her Mothers' Day speech in the morning
papers, acceded not unwillingly.
  Not that that was what Mrs. Swoffer had come for; she

said it was just a flower she wanted to gather on the way. A rose with the dew on it—she took off her glasses and wiped them, as if to show where the dew had come from. "You speak for so *many* of us," she breathed, and recovered Pauline's hand for another pressure.

But she *had* come for the children, all the same; and that was really coming for the mothers, wasn't it? Only she wanted to reach the mothers through the children—reversing the usual process. Mrs. Swoffer said she believed in reversing almost everything. Standing on your head was one of the most restorative physical exercises, and she believed it was the same mentally and morally. It was a good thing to stand one's *soul* upside down. And so she'd come about the children. . . .

The great Teacher, Alvah Loft—she supposed Mrs. Manford knew about *him*? No? She was surprised that a woman like Mrs. Manford—"one of our beacon-lights"—hadn't heard of Alvah Loft. She herself owed everything to him. No one had helped her as he had: he had pulled her out of the very depths of scepticism. But didn't Mrs. Manford know his books, even: "Spiritual Vacuum-Cleaning" and "Beyond God?"

Pauline had grown a little listless while the children were to the fore. She would help, of course! lend her name; subscribe. But that string had been so often twanged that it gave out rather a deadened note whereas the name of a new Messiah immediately roused her. "Beyond God" was a tremendous title: she would get Maisie to telephone for the books at once. But what exactly did Alvah Loft teach?

Mrs. Swoffer's eye-glasses flashed with inspiration. "He doesn't teach: he absolutely refuses to be regarded as a *teacher*. He says there are too many already. He's an Inspiration Healer. What he does is to *act* on you—on your spirit. He simply relieves you of your frustrations." [Edith Wharton, *Twilight Sleep,* D. Appleton & Co., Bk. II, 11. Copyright 1927 Edith Wharton; renewal copyright 1955 William R. Tyler. Quoted by permission.]

One recognizes an emigrant great-granddaughter of Mrs. Chadband. Indeed a good deal of the satire tends towards this kind of farcical exaggeration. The prose, if less subtle than in the early novels, is still full of liveliness in building up Edith Wharton's personal vision of her cruder material. She clearly felt that the life of New York Society had reached a level of absurdity that demanded such treatment. The quotations also introduce the principal character, Mrs. Dexter Manford, and the specific theme, symbolized by the title, which is the controlling idea of the book. The stability, the *modus vivendi*, toward which the characters strive involves in every case an escape from ordinary reality or an evasion of responsibility. It is a sort of logical conclusion of old New York's genteel avoidance of unpleasantness without the moral implications formerly involved. The euphemism for a maternity home is merely an extreme verbal case of this. Everyone is trying to get away from something, especially himself. A succession of faith-healers, that characteristic American phenomenon already diagnosed by Sinclair Lewis,[1] provide different methods by which the troubled individual can exorcise the difficulties of living with his or her—especially her—fellow human beings, the Mahatma who prescribes "mental deep-breathing" and eurythmics, Alva Loft—already illustrated—a brisk commercial type, and finally Gobine, the "scientific initiate" who "unveils the soul." The only religious ideas that mean anything to a large section of Society are represented by this vague and debilitated optimism that provides a shortcut away from any suggestion of difficulty, let alone evil or suffering. In Pauline Manford's circle this exotic quackery is easily blended with relics of Puritanism, reduced now to mere good-natured interference with other people and general prudishness. We visualize clearly

. . , the audience of bright elderly women, with snowy hair, eurythmic movements, and finely-wrinkled over-massaged faces on which a smile of glassy benevolence set like their

---

1. In *Babbitt*, 1923, but of course exposed more spectacularly in *Elmer Gantry*, also 1927.

rimless pince-nez. They were all inexorably earnest, aimlessly kind and fathomlessly pure; and all rather too well-dressed, except the "prominent woman" of the occasion, who usually wore dowdy clothes, and had steel-rimmed spectacles and straggling wisps of hair. Whatever the question dealt with, these ladies always seemed to be the same, and always advocated with equal zeal Birth Control and unlimited maternity, free love or the return to the traditions of the American home; and neither they nor Mrs. Manford seemed aware that there was anything contradictory in these doctrines. All they knew was that they were determined to force certain persons to do things that those persons preferred not to do. Nona glancing down the serried list, recalled a saying of her mother's former husband, Arthur Wyant: "Your mother and her friends would like to teach the whole world how to say its prayers and brush its teeth." [*Twilight Sleep,* Bk. I, 1. Quoted by permission.]

Edith Wharton achieves a brilliant farcically ironic exposure of the whole moral and intellectual muddle when she makes Pauline Manford read the opening section of her speech for the Birth Control banquet at the Mothers' Meeting and carry the occasion to a triumphant conclusion. Pauline Manford is a complex creation. She is a wealthy heiress from Exploit in the Middle West who has built up a considerable position in New York, not only as a philanthropist of ceaseless organization but also as a patroness of the arts and a hostess—"the year when she had had to read Proust, learn a new dance step, master oriental philosophy . . ."—on a Vanderbilt scale. Every hour of her day is regulated and her family call her boudoir the "office." She has every gadget that money can buy and is a master of business and domestic detail. Offsetting her efficiency as an organizer of the public sides of life, Pauline Manford is inept in her personal relations; she is indeed, as Mrs. Swoffer says, "frustrated" and compensates for it in a very usual way, magnified to mock-heroic proportions. With her children and with her husband she is ill at ease, though always poised, and enthusiastically substitutes the public gesture, the gift of an expensive present, or the arrangement of a holiday, for emotional contact and mutual adjustment. A day in New York is a great relief after a few days in the country. She is, in short, a millionaire *déraciné*, forever trying to hold a position in a society where fixed positions have almost disappeared and to wish away anything that reminds her of her helplessness.

Dexter Manford, her second husband, who comes from Minnesota and is a lawyer of distinction, is a more common type. He is a moral as well as a social study. After a period of fascination, he has reached what can but be called a state of mute acceptance of his position in Pauline Manford's social prison without bars. He maintains high professional and social standards of behavior and he is devoted to his daughter, Nona, and his stepson, Jim Wyant, but he characteristically lacks both general culture and self-knowledge, and these deficiencies eventually create the circumstances for his own disintegration in the "Twilight" world. He has his own angle on one side of his wife's life:

> The philanthropy was what he most hated: all these expensive plans for moral forcible feeding, for compelling everybody to be cleaner, stronger, healthier and happier than they would have been by the unaided light of Nature. The longing to get away into a world where men and women sinned and begot, lived and died, as they chose, without the perpetual intervention of optimistic millionaires, had become so strong that he sometimes felt the chain habit would snap with his first jerk.
>
> That was what had secretly drawn him to Jim's wife. She was the one person in his group to whom its catchwords meant absolutely nothing. The others, whatever their private omissions or indulgences, dressed up their selfish cravings in the same wordy altruism. [*Twilight Sleep,* Bk. II, 15. Quoted by permission.]

The kind of evasion represented by the healers he merely despises. But, though he sees his danger at one point, he nevertheless drifts gradually from a protective and paternal to a lover's attitude to his stepson's wife; he escapes from the moribund social routine and from the responsibilities of a husband and father, in which he believes, along the road of the jazz addicts and ends in disaster. He is not a subtle type but his progress is presented with admirable insight, especially in the account of his vehement desire to "rescue" Lita, which even arouses vague misgivings in his wife. The precarious and disintegrating quality of the social world inhabited by Mr. and Mrs. Manford is exposed to more good-humored scorn in the description, early in the book, of a dinner and ball that they give for the Marchesa di San Fedele, Pauline Manford's cousin by her first husband. One sees the boredom amid the luxury, especially for the tired husband after a day at the office, the breakdown of forms when the after dinner procession of men and women breaks up at the gates of the lift—only the Marchesa mounts the grand staircase on her host's arm—and the final collapse when Pauline Manford discovers that her family, including her husband, have all gone elsewhere before the supper.

The stability of the Manford family circle, such as it is, is threatened by two dangers. The enemy from without is the Marchesa, who has the brilliantly ironic name of Amalasuntha, a modern Queen of the Goths preying financially on the New World and likely to be followed by a son who may bring family destruction as well. The enemy within is Lita, the wife of Jim Wyant. She is Edith Wharton's representative of the Bright Young Things, as they were called in London, a study of egotism and irresponsibility blended into complete anarchism, and a characteristic social menace. Little as there is to be said in favor of the Manford world as stage-managed by Pauline, there is much less to be said for Lita's chaotic existence. She is caught in a vicious circle of escapism, first from conventions and then from one thrill to another; "Oh, children—but I am bored!" is a recurrent motif. The chief domestic preoccupation of the Manfords is to preserve Jim's marriage, which in the circumstances can be little more than a piece of meaningless sentimentality and a temporary avoidance of inevitable unpleasantness.

The positive values in this world of evasion and futility are represented by Nona Manford and, to some extent, by Arthur Wyant. Pauline Manford's first husband, Arthur Wyant, known in the family as mother's "Exhibit A," is a very decayed relic of old New York. His standards of gentlemanly behavior have declined into a mere evasion of unpleasantness also, but he has an important function in the pattern both as an ally of Nona and also on his own. However, it is Nona who is the real positive, and she is decidedly not part of old New York. To some extent she is part of the Jazz Age, but more from the habits of her set and generation than from inclination. Though she admires her mother, she cannot take part in her altruistic activities and she discusses the family complications amusingly with her stepfather; with her own very real and unideal love affair with a married man on her hands, she is at nineteen both extremely sophisticated and also frank and generous. Edith Wharton presents her as seeing beyond the outlook of the times:

> That was the new idea of marriage, the view of Nona's contemporaries; it had been her own a few hours since. Now, seeing it in operation, she wondered if it still were. It was one thing to theorize on the detachability of human beings, another to watch them torn apart by the bleeding roots. The botanist who had recently discovered that plants were susceptible to pain, and that transplanting was a major operation—might he not, if he turned his attention to modern men and women, find the same thing to be still true of a few of them? [*Twilight Sleep*, Bk. II, 17. Quoted by permission.]

Dexter Manford has earlier realized that she is as "firm as
a rock," and the words already quoted about "the best new
way of being decent" put her firmly in the center of the
comic pattern.

The steadily developing effort of the older generation to
wish and cajole and bribe away the disruptive efforts of
the younger and more openly egotistical and unscrupulous
escapists is brought to a characteristic climax in Book III
of the novel. Pauline Manford organizes a family escape
from each other and their problems in the form of separate
holidays. Cedarledge, the Manford country home, is a vast
and splendid creation, all exaggerated to the point of satire
—one can watch Edith Wharton, creator of houses and
gardens, overdoing everything—and the departure of
Pauline Manford from New York is indeed a "tumul-
tuous" scene; nearly every strand of the plot, social, family
and cultural, is displayed in a passage of wild satiric farce:

> "Here's another batch of bills passed by the architect, Mrs.
> Manford. And he asks if you'd mind—"
> "Yes, yes; draw another cheque for five thousand, Maisie,
> and send it to me with the others to be signed."
> "And the estimates for the new orchid-house. The contrac-
> tor says building-materials are going up again next week,
> and he can't guarantee, unless you telephone at once—"
> "Has madame the jewel-box? I put it under the rug myself,
> with madame's motor-bag."
> "Thank you, Cecile. Yes, it's here."
> "And is the Maison Herminie to deliver the green and gold
> teagown here or—"
> "Here are the proofs of the Birth Control speech, Mrs.
> Manford. If you could just glance over them in the motor,
> and let me have them back tonight—"
> "The Marchesa, madam, has called up to ask if you and
> Mr. Manford can receive her at Cedarledge for the next
> week-end—"
> "No, Powder; say no. I'm dreadfully sorry—"
> "Very good, madam. I understand it was to bring a favour-
> able answer from the Cardinal—"

"Oh: very well. I'll telephone from Cedarledge—"

"Please, madam, Mr. Wyant's just telephoned—"

"Mr. Arthur Wyant and Mr. James were to have started for Georgia last night."

"Yes, madam; but Mr. James was detained by business, and now Mr. Arthur Wyant asks if you'll please ring up before they leave tonight."

"Very well. (What can have happened. Nona? You don't know?) Say I've started for Cedarledge, Powder; I'll ring up from there. Yes; that's all."

"Mrs. Manford, wait! Here are two more telegrams, and a special—"

"Take care, Maisie; you'll slip and break your leg. . . ."

"Yes, but Mrs. Manford! The special is from Mrs. Swoffer. She says the committee have just discovered a new genius, and they're calling an emergency meeting for tomorrow afternoon at three, and couldn't you possibly—"

"No, no, Maisie—I can't! Say I've left—" [*Twilight Sleep,* Bk. III, 20. Quoted by permission.]

All her organizing power has gone into the arrangements and she enjoys a last show of triumph, but the description of Lita's arrival with Dexter Manford, with its suggestions of lover, father, and straying husband combined, has ominous undertones:

"There's the dogwood! Look! Never seen it in bloom here before, have you? It's one of our sights." He had counted a good deal on the effect of the dogwood. "Well, here we are—Jove, but it's good to be here! Why, child, I believe you've been asleep. . . ." He lifted her, still half-drowsing from the motor—

And now, the illuminated threshold, Powder, the footmen, the inevitable stack of letters—and Pauline. [*Twilight Sleep,* Bk. III, 20. Quoted by permission.]

The atmosphere is indeed continuously ominous and we watch Dexter Manford and Lita becoming more and more involved with each other and Lita displaying further stretches of egotism and silliness. Suddenly the painful and ugly side of reality is made inescapably plain to all in

Arthur Wyant's attempted murder of Manford in the arms
of his—Arthur Wyant's—son's wife. One might take it as a
last effort by the chivalry and the Puritanism of old New
York in alliance. It is a desperate and futile gesture, but
shows that Wyant still has a sense of human values in his
effete gentility. The irony cuts both ways. Arthur Wyant
has ruined himself, but of course the Manford world is also
in ruins. They can no longer deceive even themselves; they
are helpless and drifting individuals, who have betrayed
each other. The only escape now is literally in flight—the
conventional panacea of a foreign holiday. Nona is given
the last word; she would like to escape into "a convent
where nobody believes in anything." The sudden upsurge
of Puritan anti-popery that the reference arouses in Mrs.
Manford is, after her plans to entertain a cardinal, the
final exposure of her religiosity. But, though it is a fitting
dismissal of so much hocus-pocus and selfishness, as a positive comment it can only mean an escape into a lost paradise, before either good or evil were known, or mere
nonsense. Nona is also defeated, at least for the moment
It is another stalemate comic ending. *Twilight Sleep* has
certain weak features. There are thin places in the prose—
"whirls and thrills" as a description of young fashionable
life, and some unironical sentimentality in the dialogue—
"old dad" is a distressing expression even if it is authentic.
But as a whole it is a remarkably consistent piece of satire
on a community and its home-bred and purely destructive
rebels. Nona is an interesting creation. Percy Lubbock[2]
tells us of Edith Wharton's great capacity for getting on
with young people during her later years and Nona must
embody the intuitions drawn from many frank conversa-
tions. She has inherited her father's pioneer vitality together with a basic sense of responsibility and seriousness
from her mother, and she can appreciate the traditions of

2. *Portrait of Edith Wharton*, p. 182.

old New York. Young as she is, and appropriately young, she represents a combination of free intelligence and human sympathy, which Edith Wharton seems to have felt were needed to re-create a genuine society in which the individual could find fulfillment.

III

In one sense *The Children,* 1928, carries on from that point. They are the offspring of the socially anarchic younger millionaires and derelict aristocrats, beginning again from scratch. Their situation and their behavior constitute a finally damning criticism of the world of their immediate elders. The novel is again satiric comedy with several levels of complexity, social, moral, and psychological, the psychological interest being considerable. Edith Wharton has followed what is for her an unusual pattern of two plots, interlocked in the first instance by sheer accident but, in the development, interlocked most significantly at every level. Looked at separately, the story of the children with its tendency to farce is consistent and satisfying while the story of the adults is sometimes uncertain and perhaps not completely objectified.

Book I opens with Martin Boyne, an engineer born in old New York Society, on his way to Italy to see Mrs. Rose Sellars, who is now free of an unloved husband. She is said to have been a woman of very great charm, but Boyne finds a letter from her "a trifle mincing and self-conscious," and the letter also effects, for the reader, a placing of him. One sees in fact another version of the Darrow-Anna Leath situation, the revival of a love affair in later life. The children have the problems one might expect in the circumstances, and the eldest and most precocious, Judith, has become "mother" to the others. Percy Lubbock has also remarked on Edith Wharton's skill in portraying children; we have seen this in the earlier books where they

are given such significant roles. She was not at all a maternal woman but she had "the gift," in a friend's words, "of
treating children as normal human beings."[3] This partly
explains her success. She presents the little Wheaters to us,
as they painfully present themselves to Boyne, as a collection of rootless individuals, who inhabit Palace Hotels
and *wagons-lits* and lack all traditions of family life, but
who nonetheless try to keep together as a tiny self-
contained community. They represent the basic herd instinct divorced from all conventions and moral ideas. They
are determined to keep out of a life which is mean, nasty,
brutish, and often short, but they have not got very far
on their own. They are not nice children; they are childish
and unpleasantly precocious by turns; they are selfish,
quarrelsome, lying, and thieving. Edith Wharton has en-
visaged the situation with great insight. It has also something in common with William Golding's vision in *The
Lord of the Flies,* but Edith Wharton is not attempting
a self-contained allegory of reversion; instead she offers a
social analogue. The grown-ups are still there, but after
all no community is completely isolated, even a camp of
displaced persons, and these are miniature displaced
persons, usually, however, without economic problems.
Through Boyne's eyes we see in Venice what the adult
world where they were born is like. Cliffe Wheater, the
father of some of them, and his wife live a life of pointless
amusement, in revolt against conventions that in fact no
longer really exist. Judith tells Boyne more about the less
savory side of the little Wheaters and what they know, and
she emerges as an older version of Maisie who, in spite of
it all, preserves a basic innocence of intention and sense
of responsibility. One sees both aspects of the situation,
the child-woman in Judith and Boyne's ambiguous attitude, in the following dialogue:

---

3. *Ibid.,* p. 138.

"Go to school? Me? But when, I'd like to know? There'll always be some of the children left to look after. Why, I shall be too old for school before Chip is anywhere near Terry's age. And besides I never mean to leave the children—never!" She brought the word out with the shrill emphasis he had already heard in her voice when her flock had to be protected or reproved. "We've all sworn that," she added. "We took an awful oath one day at Biskra that we'd never be separated again, no matter what happened. . . ."

"But now that all the children are safely with your own people, couldn't you let the oath take care of itself, and think a little of what's best for you?"

"She raised her eyes with a puzzled stare which made them seem as young as Zinnie's. "You'd like me to go to school?"

He returned the look with one of equal gravity. "Most awfully."

Her colour rose a little. "Then I should like to."

"Well, then—"

She shook her head and her flush faded. "I don't suppose you'll ever understand—you or anybody. How could I leave the children now? I've got to get them off to Switzerland in another fortnight: this is no place for Terry. And suppose Mr. Ormerod decides he won't come with us—"

"Won't come with you? But it's precisely what he's been engaged to do.!"

She gave an impatient shrug like her mother's and turned on Boyne a little face sharp with interrogation. "Well, then suppose it was mother who didn't want him to?"

"Your mother? Why, child, it was she who found him. She knows all about him; she—"

"She jolly well likes doing Venice with him . . . I suppose you think I oughtn't to say things like that about mother—but what am I to do, when they're true, and there's no one but you that I can say them to?" [Edith Wharton, *The Children*, D. Appleton & Co., Bk. I, 7. Copyright 1928 Edith Wharton; renewal copyright 1955 William R. Tyler. Quoted by permission.]

When Boyne leaves them to continue on his way to meet Rose Sellars we get a complete contrast in a return to social forms. Boyne feels that he is "punctual and conscientious" in a "clockless and conscienceless world";

Edith Wharton again makes the breakdown of even the daily routine of fashionable leisured life, as she had known it, indicative of the whole disintegration. Boyne is already torn between Judith and Rose Sellars but, wanting stability as much as do the little Wheaters, he cannot separate himself from his social and emotional past. Rose Sellars would appear to resemble the author in appearance and one senses, more strongly than in *The Reef*, a failure in objectivity at this point. Indeed the account of the relationship with Boyne tends to the sentimental and even the slightly religiose, for example in "his passion lay with folded wings," an image used in *The Reef* twenty years before. Too many things are described as "perfect"; there is again a lack of human depth and warmth. It is very much like the peaceful parts of the earlier novel, when the Wheater problem, with its multiple and sordid implications, intrudes itself upon them.

The primitive life of the children and the highly civilized but secluded life of Boyne and Rose Sellars are now closely interwoven and made to react on each other. The little Wheaters suddenly arrive in Cortina—on stolen funds—and one learns that the Wheater parents are separating again and, put with a typically ironical shift into childishness, that mother's friend "Sally Money" is a serious problem. Rose Sellars, as she herself says, and as one might expect "didn't know there were such people" and she can hardly be impressed either by Judith's sophistication or by her naivety. On the other hand Judith's comments on Rose Sellars and Boyne are remarkably mature:

> "If she's not as old as mother, and you've never noticed how she's dressed, you must be in love with her," Judith went on, as if his last words had not made the least impression on her.
> "I don't see what difference it makes if I am or not," he retorted, beginning to lose his temper. "The point is that she happens to be one of the kindest and most sensible women I

know—" "That's what men always think," said Judith thoughtfully. [*The Children*, Bk. II, 12. Quoted by permission.]

When Boyne, who is committed to the children, goes to Venice to treat with Mr. and Mrs. Wheater, the satiric feeling has a vehemence corresponding to the indignation of Boyne and Rose Sellars. We are given a contemptuous picture of selfishness, irresponsibility, and dullness. The new social circus on the Lido has more vitality than the vulgarized formalism of the old "House of Mirth" or even the hotel life of European resorts in Undine Spragg's day, but the vitality is rather bogus. The smartness is crude and the amusements stereotyped in a new way. The characters are ignorant about everything except the details of each other's personal lives; one agrees that "the pure in heart have so many more things to talk about." The satire moves easily from ironic observation to the straight condemnation of "bloodless savagery."

The two stories have become a carefully balanced record of conflicting loyalties and Edith Wharton's powers of suggesting ambiguous emotional atmosphere and states of inadequate self-knowledge have plenty of scope. When he tells Judith about the engagement, we see how unaware of his own feelings Boyne still is. She is as usual very down to earth and he, to hide his embarrassment from himself, has to tell himself very loudly that she is only a child. Boyne is faced with his choice and it becomes plain that he is not sure what the alternative to Rose Sellars is:

"I can't come to-morrow."
He was conscious that she was making an intense effort to steady her quivering nerves. "Martin . . . I don't want to be unreasonable . . ."
"You're never unreasonable," he said patiently.
"You mean it might have been better if I were!" she flashed back, crimsoning . . .
"All I care for is to know the truth. . . ."

"I'm telling you the truth."

"You may think you are. But the truth is something very different—something you're not conscious of yourself, perhaps . . . not clearly . . ."

"I believe I'm telling you the whole truth."

"That when I ask you to choose between me and the Wheater children, you choose the Wheater children—out of philanthropy?"

"I didn't say out of philanthropy. I said I didn't know. . . ."

"If you don't know, I do. You're in love with Judith Wheater, and you're still in love with me." [*The Children*, Bk. III, 22. Quoted by permission.]

After this delicately dramatized analysis of divided emotional states, the situation is treated as tragedy:

His eyes rested on her profile, so thin, drawn, blood-less, that a fresh pang shot through him. He had often mocked at himself as a man who, in spite of all his wanderings, had never had a real adventure; but now he saw that he himself had been one, had been Rose Sellars's Great Adventure, the risk and the enchantment of her life. While she had continued, during the weary years of her marriage, to be blameless, exemplary, patient and heroically gay, the thought of Boyne was storing up treasures for her which she would one day put out her hand and take—no matter how long she might have to wait. Her patience, Boyne knew, was endless—it was as long as her hair. She had trained herself to go on waiting for happiness, day after day, month after month, year after year with the same air of bright unruffled vigilance, like a tireless animal waiting for its prey. One day her prey, her happiness, would appear, and she would snap it up; and on that day there would be no escape from her. . . .

It was terrible, it was hideous, to be picturing her distress as something grasping and predatory; it was more painful to be entering so acutely into her feelings while a central numbness paralysed his own. All around this numbness there was a great margin of pity and of comprehension; but he knew this was not the region by way of which he could reach her. She who had always lived the life of reason would never forgive him if he called upon her reason now. [*The Children*, Bk. III, 22. Quoted by permission.]

The strongly critical implications of the images that convey Boyne's vision have a decidedly unsettling effect on the reader's response. We are clearly meant to see and sympathize with both points of view here, but nevertheless, and allowing for Boyne's being the perceiving and mediating consciousness, one feels that there is more animus against Rose Sellars in the passage than the book as a whole intends. As with Anna Leath, one feels that there is an element of self-criticism; Edith Wharton has created a character rather like herself, as she knew she really was but not as she knew other people might well think she was. Like Anna Leath, Rose Sellars is a very fastidious woman who has lived a sheltered life; as Edith Wharton puts it, she is "not a denier, but that rarer being, a chooser." She attempts a reasonable compromise solution of their problems. Boyne's dilemma is that he is torn between a love that he takes for granted, despite his idealization, to the extent of expecting far more than compromise, and his fascination with a sophisticated child of nature. One may say that Rose Sellars has the moral advantage in terms of both generosity and good sense, but nevertheless that does not make her a more suitable wife for Boyne. One comes back to the artistic problem of intention and direction of sympathies.

We are now given the final stages of Boyne's "adventure" with the children. He settles down to a rather regressive, would-be avuncular existence, both he and they clinging to the bit of stable life they have. He is subjected to a pretty thorough ironical exposure. He becomes conscious at long last that he is in love with Judith and also realizes that she has never dreamt of such a situation. Now that his engagement to Rose Sellars has been broken off, he realizes that he valued her as a relief from the Wheaters, but he also realizes that his idealization of her has never been the equivalent of the passion he now feels. The escape from these dilemmas can only be the conventional refuge in work, Boyne being a portrait of a conventional type of man with old New York standards of an honorable life; Newland Archer had acted similarly in his generation. He and Rose Sellars form a criticism of the promiscuities of the Lido, but their own inadequacies have been made plain—Mrs. Sellars's at least by implication, even if they are not consistently admitted by the author. The children with their gregariousness and their amorality are both an unhappy product, and, as a microcosm, also a criticism of their elders' muddledom. We are left with the human welter, as Edith Wharton often calls it, and the feeling that "a tawdry cheapness shall outlast our days"; there is no Nona Manford in *The Children*.

IV

Edith Wharton's later stories are not up to the standard of her earlier work, and in four volumes, 1926-36, only a very few are worth attention. Among quite a number of slick magazine treatments of situations that she might in earlier life have made morally and psychologically interesting, *Atrophy* stands out for its ironic blend of the comic and the pathetic. A spinster contrives by apparently conventional but in reality pointedly ambiguous conversation to keep a married woman visitor away from her dying brother. To the woman the motive appears to be condemnation of adultery, to the reader a more deeply underlying combination of envy and frustration is perceptible.

The remaining noteworthy stories are satire or comedy of the kind we have been considering. *After Holbein* reads almost as an indictment of the whole New York social order, old and new; the date of the action could be prewar or postwar. It is a truly devastating satire, culminating in macabre horror, on formal entertaining in the grand style as practiced by the very wealthy of old and newer New York:

Hundreds, no, thousands of dinners (on gold plate, of course, and with orchids, and all the delicacies that were out of season), had been served in that vast pompous dining-room, which one had only to close one's eyes to transform into a railway buffet for millionaires, at a big junction, before the invention of restaurant trains. . . .

There was really no reason why that kind of standardized entertaining should ever cease; a performance so undiscriminating, so undifferentiated, that one could almost imagine, in the hostess's tired brain, all the dinners she had ever given merging into one Gargantuan pyramid of food and drink, with the same faces, perpetually the same faces, gathered stolidly about the same gold plate.

Thank heaven, Anson Warley had never conceived of social values in terms of mass and volume. It was years since he had dined at Mrs. Jaspar's. [Edith Wharton, "After Holbein," in *Certain People*, D. Appleton & Co. Copyright 1930 Edith Wharton; renewal copyright 1958 William R. Tyler. Quoted by permission.]

We then proceed to the Dance of Death as Warley, having gone out to dinner and lost his own memory, presents himself at her house. Mrs. Jaspar, who is suffering from softening of the brain, is shown going through her regular simulacrum of the dinner parties of her prime; it is a hideous and ridiculous performance that reduces the supreme social ritual to imbecile gropings, an attack on the kind of millionaire splendor that is criticized, though less roughly handled, in the prewar novels and later in *A Backward Glance*. One may wonder for a moment whether the animus is partly personal. It is an obvious description of the senility of Mrs. William Astor, who died in 1908, and it would appear that she did not make a habit of receiving Mrs. Edward Wharton.[4]

Roman Fever is a very light little comedy that can be taken as a kind of farewell skit on the decorum of the great days. Two smart middle-aged mothers, each "the modest

---

4. See *The Vanderbilt Feud*, p. 170, which suggests this.

appendage of a salient daughter," spend the afternoon "reminiscing" on the terrace of a restaurant overlooking the Palatine. Two personalities are most elegantly revealed in a series of confessions that put Daisy Miller's escapades, in however bad taste, quite in the shade. After drawing so many themes and types of character from the Society of the city of her birth and making so much of its values in morals, cultural interests, manners, and customs, it is very appropriate that Edith Wharton, as the connoisseur of "good talk," should end her presentation of it with this glimpse of an unexpected kind of sophistication.

9 The Writer and the Community

I

On approaching the end of Edith Wharton's work, it seems natural to say something of her ideas on the art of the novel, and it is the more appropriate to do so at this point because in the twenties she was herself engaged in summing up what she had been doing and in considering her relationship to the tradition of the novel in her own country. She was never a journalist, whether from taste or absence of necessity, and we have very few prewar reviews or articles. Her review of Leslie Stephen's *George Eliot*[1] is, despite her admiration for the subject, insignificant. Her review of Sturgis's *Belchamber*,[2] on the other hand, is of considerable interest in that her remarks on Edwardian Society are closely related to what she had just written about American Society in *The House of Mirth* and to what she wrote about it in her preface thirty years later, and also because *Belchamber* may be linked in other ways to her last novel, *The Buccaneers*. Her first more general essay, "The Criticism of Fiction,"[3] foreshadows Virginia Woolf's comments on the immaturity of English 19th-century fiction and goes on to stress the organic quality of great novels in a manner clearly indebted to James.

The Writing of Fiction, 1925, belongs to the doldrum period of creative production which, as we have seen, pre-

1. *The Bookman* 15, May, 1902.
2. *Ibid.* 21, May, 1905.
3. *The Times Literary Supplement* 14, May, 1914.

ceded the writing of *Twilight Sleep*. It is a stock-taking of her own art and of her reading of her predecessors. She had behind her, as the first elaboration of the ideas of James's Prefaces, Percy Lubbock's *Craft of Fiction*. Edith Wharton also writes as a follower of James and with her own problems as a practicing novelist very much in mind, and like James himself she is concerned with the value of novels in terms of their vitality and seriousness. Her first chapter makes it quite clear, through her comments on Stendhal and Balzac, that for her the essential qualities of fiction are, as we have already deduced, the social relations of the characters presented in all concreteness, and the moral purport of the whole story. She rejects the mere "slice of life" and the mere "stream of consciousness" as material and method respectively, on the grounds that, in the one case, the representation of life is liable, except in the hands of genius, to get bogged down in pointless detail, and that, in the other, rational behavior is normally to be expected from men and women at "crucial moments." There would seem to be a certain naivety, which is surprising, about this last assertion, though one can agree with her main argument about value residing in literature that presents life comprehensively as readily as one can with her discussion of stylization as the basis of art. Her more detailed discussion of the novel is of mixed quality. The oddest thing in these chapters is her argument that *The Kreutzer Sonata* is more objective in treatment than *Adolphe*. Her main line of argument is, of course, Jamesian, and her criticism of *The Awkward Age* as lost in its own convention of dialogue is made on Jamesian grounds. She is advocating, as she practiced in her own work, carefully selective conventions aimed at verisimilitude of total effect; *The Golden Bowl* she finds incredible in certain important aspects of its telling. She writes at some length on problems of the use of dialogue, which she says "should be reserved for culminating moments"; on the problem of indicating the passage of time, in which she was both exact and unobtrusive—apart from dovetailing in antecedents, she rarely modified chronology; and on the problem of the point of view, which is always most judiciously chosen and made significant. She does not really add anything to what the Master had said or implied on this last aspect. The importance of making scene and character "visible," which was one of her fundamental principles, is discussed in what is on the whole a rather inconclusive article in *The Yale Review*.[4] One comes back to her chief criterion of meticulous selection and planning of material to achieve artistic unity and lifelikeness of final result, and one wonders how far she had considered the nature and effect of the comic exaggeration of a great deal of *The Custom of the Country,* not to mention the comic or heroic modes of other novelists. She apologizes for repeating "that all art is re-presentation—the giving back in conscious form of the shapeless raw material of experience . . . 'stylization,' " but later says "Verisimilitude is the truth of art, and any convention that hinders the illusion is obviously in the wrong place." She appears to be having it both ways, as do James and Percy Lubbock, but more careful consideration shows that this is not really the case. She was in fact an intelligent critic, although not in advance of her time, and like them she means by verisimilitude an interpretation of reality in reading which one can suspend one's disbelief. Edith Wharton belongs with the distinguished company who during the last fifty years have worked toward precision in critical terminology and standards of critical evaluation. Her chapter on Proust exemplifies her powers.

"The Great American Novel"[5] and certain pages in *A*

4. *The Yale Review* 18, n.s., 1929.
5. *Ibid.* 16, n.s., 1927.

Backward Glance should keep those critics quiet, or at least compel many qualifications in their judgments, who in recent years have accused Edith Wharton not merely of a hostile attitude to American life and culture beyond the range of New York but of actual ignorance of, and indifference to, American writers. Her ironical account of the attitude of her parents' circle toward Melville and others should indicate her own different opinion. Her high estimate of Hawthorne is unequivocal and her rejection of both the "lavender-scented New England" and the "chivalrous South" of 19th-century sentimental tradition went along with an interest in the earlier realists, such as Robert Grant and Frank Norris. She points out the irony of Lewis's satiric picture of *Main Street*'s being made a norm of suitable American subject matter. She was, of course, engaged in combating the growing demand of the time that American novelists should confine themselves to American subject matter, which she points out was not a limitation that other countries wished to impose on their writers; she did not realize its significance in terms of a new kind of national self-consciousness, but was concerned only with the dangers of a reviving provincialism. She is concerned at the dullness of the subject matter in a life reduced to a "dead level of prosperity," good plumbing, and "vapid benevolence"; at the not merely "middle class," which she had known in old New York, but "middling" quality of life; and at the impossibility of developing complex thought or portraying a "social and educated being" amid this mediocre standardization. All she asks for the American novelist is freedom to find his subjects where he chooses. She sees no special virtue in cosmopolitanism, but the writer, she says, needs a subject "in which there is something corresponding to something within himself." The general principle seems the acme of common sense and one would hardly dispute her estimates of her predecessors and her contemporaries, senior and junior. It is curious and ironical that James said in her early days that she "should be tethered to native pastures"[6]—but that was just after *The Valley of Decision*—and that forty years later Percy Lubbock wondered whether she would not, in spite of herself, have been a happier and greater novelist on "the frontier."[7] Such speculation is not, however, very fruitful. Edith Wharton did not write well of Hanaford, but her Middle-West characters in contact with New Yorkers are vivid and powerful creations. It was dramatic contrasts that aroused her creative genius, the conflicts between "social order and individual appetites." She knew what she was doing and she kept to what she found congenial; which artistically successful novelist has done otherwise? Her article came out in the year of *Twilight Sleep*. After that last long satiric look at Society, she turned her attention to a new and specifically American subject, the young and unsophisticated writer of the day coming to terms with the New York literary world and with life in general. She had already tried a study of a young writer of her own generation in *Literature;*[8] the earlier part, except for the transposition of sex and place —little girl in West Twenty-third Street into little boy in a rectory on the Hudson, is closely autobiographical, but she did not carry her treatment of spiritual awakening and rebellion very far before abandoning it, and the fragment lacks irony and objectivity. To attempt this theme for the younger, and so different, generation was a considerable undertaking for a novelist of such distinctive and well-established literary habits, and the attempt deserves a careful study, especially in view of the fact that Mrs. Wharton seems to have looked upon these two novels as among her

---

6. *The Letters,* 1:404.
7. *Portrait of Edith Wharton,* p. 219.
8. Fragment in Yale University Library.

own favorites; the others were *The Custom of the Country, Summer* and *The Children.*[9]

II

Edith Wharton's two novels, *Hudson River Bracketed,* 1929 and *The Gods Arrive,* 1932, combine a treatment of the *Roderick Hudson* theme of the young artist precipitated into the world of his fellows and the *education sentimentale* theme in a wider sense. The title of the first epitomizes the general theme of provincialism; it was an early 19th-century rural style of architecture with many wooden balconies and projecting joists and rafters, which A. J. Downing in his fascinating books[10] classes with the great styles of the world. *Hudson River* is solemn and rather dull. Edith Wharton's powers of irony are usually in abeyance once again and one cannot take the hero as seriously as he is offered. It may be true that her picture of the Middle West is something of a caricature, but one should point out in defence of the author's attitude in the book as a whole that Vance Weston is presented for our whole-hearted sympathy as having all the freshness and innocent energy of the young pioneer, qualities that he keeps through all difficulties and temptations. The opening scenes with Vance (born at Advance, Mo.) as a callow youth at Euphoria, Illinois, are fairly straightforward comedy, the ingredients being his parents' rising standard of living and his grandparents' picturesque muddle. Grandma Scrimser, with her "ungirt frame," is a rather magnificent comic character who devotes her life to religious revivalism of the old-fashioned moralizing kind, while her husband is a handsome elderly lecher with a flair for Fourth-

9. See "Profile of Edith Wharton," *The Herald Tribune,* European edition, 16 November 1936.
10. *A Treatise on the Theory and Practice of Landscape Gardening, adapted to North America, 1844,* and the *Architecture of Country Houses, 1853.*

of-July oratory. Vance's first emotional crisis follows his accidental witnessing of an encounter between the old man and a notorious blonde called Floss Delaney, with whom he himself has already had an affair. It is a far cry from this mixture of vulgarity, religiosity, and squalor to the austere refinement of Northampton, Mass. The comparison is, however, far more than a formality. Whereas Roderick Hudson and Rowland Mallet, though they may both seem to us now strangely unaware of mid-19th-century developments in the visual arts, nevertheless know something of the still-dominant academic tradition, Vance Weston has no other idea of how to begin a literary career than through daily journalism. He is not blamed or criticized for this; it is simply presented to us as a sociological fact, a result of the breakdown of cultural communications in an expanding and fissiparous society. Roderick Hudson is lucky, but he gets to Rome through an ordinary family contact. Vance Weston's introduction to literary New York is far more fortuitous. This is Edith Wharton's basic situation out of which she develops her whole representative study.

Vance Weston is first given a glimpse of traditional culture by being sent to stay with his impoverished cousins, the Tracys, at Paul's Landing on the Hudson. His amazement at the lack of modern material amenities further exemplifies his inexperience. The Willows, the uninhabited but carefully preserved house in the Hudson River Bracketed style, represents an older kind of provincialism than the "Colonial style" houses of Euphoria, but it also stands for cultural tradition and social continuity; it contains a library that is Vance's first sight of a private collection of books and is his introduction to the English poets whose very names he scarcely knows. His reflection, "Why wasn't I ever told about the Past before?" sums up his isolation and rootlessness. He is next brought into contact with Heloise Spear (Halo) and her family, whose house is

really old and who represent an old-fashioned literary culture and a feckless, not to say sponging, old-fashioned
gentility. Halo Spear is a little older than Vance. She is
literary in her interests and decidedly patronizing in her
behavior, and she organizes a sort of "young poet and his
muse" relationship of a conventionally romantic, and very
naïve, kind. In all this Vance is not only the inexperienced
and unattached writer, but the solitary individual, drifting from one unconnected group to another. The Spear
family have their links with contemporary literary circles
in New York but really represent a relic of the newly
emancipated individualism of the previous age; the son
represents a kind of irresponsible individualism, without
thought for its victims, which is perennial. It is therefore
true to say, without any criticism's necessarily being implied, that Vance's contact with upper-class life is at one
remove from the traditional order of old New York, as
presented in earlier novels, and his literary career starts
from this point also. He has floundered through a sequence
of social, personal, and literary experiences and achieved
something at the end. The dedicatory scene by the Atlantic
ocean that follows is, however, pompous and theatrical in
the worst sense.

A gap of three years does not produce significant developments of character, and the rest of the story is the interplay of the adventures of Halo Spear and Vance, as each
attempts to make an individual life with its own individual
relation to tradition. Halo has married Lewis Tarrant,
another aspiring patron of letters and an interesting study
in egotism, who looks upon Vance as his own discovery.
"In a world of shifting standards" and "suffocating dis-
simulations" she clings to her own values, her conception
of the individual; though she has settled down with Tarrant, she is still full of ill-defined aspirations:

Never was a girl more in love with the whole adventure of

living, and less equipped to hold her own in it, than the
Halo Spear who had come upon Vance Weston that after-
noon . . .
She wanted a companion on the flaming ramparts: and
New York had so far failed to find her one. [Edith Wharton,
Hudson River Bracketed, D. Appleton & Co., Bk. VII, 41.
Copyright 1929 Edith Wharton; renewal copyright 1957 Wil-
liam R. Tyler. Quoted by permission.]

She has previously been too tied by genuine attachment
to her family to break away and make a separate life, but
one cannot imagine her in any emotional circumstances
corresponding to the image of the "flaming ramparts"; she
has too much in common with several of Edith Wharton's
other heroines, together with the patronizing, even maternal vein that has already been commented on. Though
this last aspect of her is presented ironically, a range of
sympathetic impulses seems to be missing from Halo, and
her more "emancipated" behavior seems in its way conventional. One is indeed often in considerable doubt about
Edith Wharton's attitude to her character.

Vance's progress and emotional education are much
more erratic. He characteristically wrecks his reunion with
the literary world because of a more romantic reunion
with his female cousin, Laura Lou Tracy; his attitude to
her represents a development in his personality beyond the
merely sensual attraction of Floss Delaney and similar
characters and the sort of tutelage he was in to Halo, but
it is still extremely adolescent and the situation is presented with sympathetic irony. His runaway marriage is a
rash gesture of independence and a minor victory for culture over provincial philistinism of yet another type. The
portrait of his rival, Bunty Hayes, is a study of amiable
vulgarity, on the upward move in a world open to all tal-
ents; he is a simpler and less-talented version of Elmer
Moffatt. The satiric description of New York's literary
community, in terms of the Loafers' Club and the Cocoa-

nut Tree Restaurant, is all a little simplified and too obviously second-hand, except for the story of the Pulsifer Prize, which has a devastating authenticity. It is Vance's one completely upper-class contact, but is no more a contact with stability than any other. Vance's life as a writer and as a man is now complicated by Laura Lou's illness and his own changed attitude to Halo. This latter relationship begins to take on an air of maturity when he attempts to make her into a mistress instead of a governess, and she now becomes extremely respectable despite her breach with Tarrant, as one would expect she might.

Vance's own career has come up against stupidity and concealed snobbery in the case of Mrs. Pulsifer, and another kind of snobbery and simple obtuseness to the movements of human feeling and results of human action in the case of Halo. In interpreting his reactions to the results of his own blundering, in situations that he does not yet fully understand, Edith Wharton conveys by implication a good deal of criticism of Halo's possessive and patronizing behavior. It is plain that at this stage both Halo and Vance—she because of conceit based on considerable, but still inadequate experience, and he because of the conceit of sheer inexperience—are a long way from coming to terms with themselves or with the fluctuating life around them.

The various groups of characters are now intermingled in a way that suggests the confused quality of the social and intellectual scene at the time. We find Vance and Laura Lou and Bunty Hayes, now an organizer of art exhibitions, circulating with the Tarrants in one more or less undifferentiated *melée,* with the old Spears, and even Mrs. Scrimser, also involved. Mrs. Scrimser's visit to New York on her "Meet God" preaching tour is good pathetic comedy; she is rather out of her depth with the "Seekers." Mr. Spear's comment, "Seems to me I've met Mrs.

Scrimser's God before—and Mrs. Scrimser too," sums up the situation.

The novel is wound up very hurriedly. Vance has developed intellectually a considerable way, particularly in his appreciation of the value of history and tradition, but his relationship to Laura Lou has never been more than sentimental and physical, his impulsiveness has never let him get beyond a start in a literary career, and he has not found a place in any social group. To some extent this is to his credit, the New York literary and social worlds being as they are shown, but on the other hand he himself does not strike one as a personality or an artist of great distinction. He is about to return to what roots he has in Euphoria when Halo reappears, and in the last paragraph he feels, for the first time, that she is emotionally dependent on him. On this new note a definite stage has been reached in his personal, if not in his artistic life.

III

The Gods Arrive is a much more lively, and on the whole better-planned production than *Hudson River*, even though the central relationship gets out of hand toward the end, and the conclusion, based on the title from Emerson, is neither realistically convincing nor symbolically consistent. The novel has a certain picaresque quality; each place and main episode, satirically treated in the rather broad outlines characteristic of Edith Wharton's later work, holds far more interest than the descriptions of the New York literary world. Vance Weston, in spite of increased maturity, still does not evoke the wholehearted sympathy that seems expected of us, and Halo even less so. Edith Wharton is more successful when she is being satiric, and Floss Delaney now emerges as a sort of latter-day Undine Spragg.

The picture of Parisian Bohemia in the twenties is lively straightforward satire. After all, Mrs. Wharton knew something of the milieu of Scott Fitzgerald and Walter Berry's relative, Harry Crosby. She was not as easily put out of countenance as is Mrs. Glaisher, her portrait of a New York millionairess who has taken up modern art rather late in life:

> As Vance watched her arrival he guessed in how many strange places that unblenching satin slipper had been set, and read, in the fixity of her smile, and the steady gaze of her small inquisitive eyes, her resolve to meet without wavering any shock that might await her. He thought of Halo's suggestion for his next novel, and was amused at the idea of depicting this determined woman, who, during an indefatigable lifetime, had seen almost everything and understood nothing. [Edith Wharton, *The Gods Arrive*, Charles Scribners's Sons, Bk. II, 13. Copyright 1932 Edith Wharton; renewal copyright 1959 William R. Tyler. Quoted by permission.]

In this kind of setting Vance gains confidence as a writer and produces a novel with a title that reminds one of Dreiser. His life with Halo, however, is complicated by the tergiversations of Lewis Tarrant and by his own waywardness. Whatever surviving moral considerations there may be in the attitude of certain people in Society to Halo's present position, Tarrant's reasons for refusing to permit divorce are purely personal; it is once again a conflict of individuals among themselves, not of individuals with a group. Vance also—as often before—is inclined to do as he likes on the impulse of the moment. Tarrant's conduct, however, brings to a head a developing trend in Vance away from his own egotism, innocent though this is, into much greater awareness of the situation of others. He feels that he ought to release Halo from any obligation to himself, which is evidence of an important stage in his sentimental education. Halo, faced with the dilemma whether to marry Vance and stabilize life for both of them or leave him for good, shows that, quite apart from legalities, she has not yet emerged from her romanticism; she can only talk vaguely of giving freedom to genius.

This lasts some time and makes possible Edith Wharton's final disposition of her characters. Vance at last returns home to the Middle West, but finds he still has no place there. Instead of the old blend of Philistinism and Puritanism of the more vigorous sort, one sees a new easy-going morality, very similar to the metropolitan kind, which seeks to make sin unnecessary rather than secretly to connive at it. Mrs. Scrimser, however, has her reservations, and her dying words, "We haven't made enough of pain," are intended to be a highly significant comment on the community all around her; but, as before, one cannot give her the full value that some aspects seem to demand and, in fact, deserve. The final attempt is now made to lift the novel to a higher plane and to say something profound about the relationship between men and women as individual human beings. Vance's retreat to a mountain camp to recuperate provides an opportunity for a spiritual awakening. He returns to Paul's Landing to refresh his impressions of the place where he feels life really began for him and finds Halo engaged on a similar project at the Willows. That old New York is still a basis for civilized life seems to be the implication; individuals need an anchorage away from the prevailing maelstrom. Vance says that he returns to Halo as a child:

> Suddenly he moved toward her with a gesture of passionate entreaty. "Don't you see, Halo—*can't* you see? I can't come back to you just because I'm at the end of everything. To any other woman—not to you. But I wasn't strong enough to go away without telling you; the only strength left to me is the strength not to pretend, or to invent lying reasons. And that's not much . . . you're different. I read something up there in the woods about God . . . or experience . . . it's the same

thing . . . being the food of the full-grown. That seemed to explain a lot to me. I'm not fit for you yet, Halo: I'm only just learning to walk. . . ."

She leaned against the mantel-piece, fighting down the old tremors in her breast; at length she gave a little laugh. "But then I shall have two children to take care of instead of one!"

He raised his eyes to her, and she moved across the room and stood before him. With a kind of tranquil gravity she lifted up her arms in the ancient attitude of prayer.

For a moment his brow kept its deep furrows of bewilderment; then he gave a start and went up to her with illuminated eyes.

"You see we belong to each other after all," she said, but as her arms sank about his neck he bent his head and put his lips to a fold of her loose dress. [*The Gods Arrive*, Bk. V, 41. Quoted by permission.]

At the end of *Hudson River,* he felt she was momentarily a child to him. Now she is very much the mother figure— in every sense—as she has often been in attitude of mind. The original situation has been allowed to evolve and Vance at least has gained a knowledge of the various overlapping groups that now make up the American and European communities. He has become a celebrated novelist and he has developed emotionally, but though certain half Gods have gone it is difficult to feel much impressed by the Gods (or Goddess) that have arrived. It is noteworthy that Halo has the last word and that Vance is a suppliant as well as a child. Halo belongs to the emancipated modern world in most respects and the Puritan tradition in her is not much more than a vague sense of having duties, but she does not quite live up to the values she is intended to represent. One is left with a feeling of dissatisfaction and also with, as has been said, considerable uncertainty as to how seriously to take it all and how clear Edith Wharton herself was about the issues raised. After so many brilliant pictures of men and women in society, even a society disintegrating, this attempt to present as it were the essence of a relationship, to do in fact the kind of thing that Lawrence had just been doing without, as she put it, using a megaphone,[13] is disappointing. But perhaps this is to be expected. One does not imply superficiality if one says that Edith Wharton needed a full social context in order to show human beings as she knew them. In her last book she set out to do something with this scope once again, but with an entirely new and original treatment.

13. See "Tendencies in Modern Fiction," *Saturday Review,* 7 April 1934.

10 Society Reconsidered

The Buccaneers, posthumously published in 1938, is unfinished, but is sufficiently rich in detail and clear in outline to be regarded as one of Edith Wharton's major works. One should place it along with *The House of Mirth* and *The Custom of the Country.* While one must be deeply grateful to Gaillard Lapsley for his editing of the novel and for his information about the long and careful attention that Edith Wharton gave to it during the last four or five years of her life, one cannot help feeling that he may be partly responsible for the undue interest that has been taken in Laura Testvalley. This, of course, is abetted by her own account in *A Backward Glance* of how the name came to her—it is strange that she did not see it as a pleasantly appropriate English place name as well as an anglicization of the Italian—but the idea of a governess-adventuress, with all its Victorian associations, has been a little too attractive to sentimentalizing propensities. Laura Testvalley does not, if one reads with a critical interest, dominate the book as it stands, and there seems no reason why Nan St. George should not have emerged even more fully as the central figure, had the novel been completed along the lines foreshadowed by the hints and pointers that exist.

It is sometimes suggested that Edith Wharton's novels, *The Age of Innocence* and *The Buccaneers,* followed by *The House of Mirth* and *The Custom of the Country,* form a simple sequence chronicling the changing forms of New York Society down to her own day. Closer consideration, however, should make one realize that only *The Age of Innocence* is a historical novel in the narrower sense. *The Buccaneers* deals with an early phase of American social climbing, that represented by the post-Civil War wealthy, but Edith Wharton was in this last work attempting much more than a piece of historical reconstruction, brilliant and varied though this aspect of the book may be. A theme emerges clearly and it is a kind of recapitulation of her work in reverse order, but adumbrating a positive and forward-looking conclusion, rather than a mere retreat into nostalgia or traditional formalism. In theme, if not as history, *The Buccaneers* begins where her novels of the 1920s, *Twilight Sleep* and *The Children,* leave off— in social anarchy. And, by involving the anarchic spirits in all their free vitality with a social system which is at once very old and very stable, it gradually works toward a vision of social reintegration with moral and intellectual concomitants, a concept of balance between ancient order and dignity and new, sincere, and unconventional individualism. This theme is presented in terms of the career of the heroine, beginning as Nan St. George, becoming the Duchess of Tintagel, and expected to end as Mrs. Guy Thwarte. There is a strong relationship to Nona Manford of *The Children* in the values and attitudes she stands for, though nothing corresponding to the sophistication of the modern heroine.

Edith Wharton's prose has lost the epigrammatic tension and much of the vivid figurative language that marks her prewar books, but in becoming more leisurely and matter-of-fact, it has not become dull. Successive groupings of characters are as "visible" as she could have wished and the old sense of irony is rejuvenated in the juxtaposition of episodes and the flair for significant detail, though there are a few places in the dialogue and in the rendering of the meditations of the characters where background material does not seem to have been quite transformed into fiction—the novel is, after all, unfinished. Description of settings is often extremely evocative without being sentimental, deliberately traditional but not commonplace.

Saratoga in the 70s, which Edith Wharton makes the setting of her opening scenes, was no longer an exclusive resort, and, as she never mentions it in *A Backward Glance,* one may perhaps conjecture that her family did not make a habit of going there. However, her picture of a no-man's land is admirably suited to the human situation displayed in it. Every feature indicates the particular phase of newly rich social uncertainty and incompleteness, at times disintegrating into chaos, which she wishes to contrast with well-tried and established traditional organization and routine. The Grand Union Hotel seems sufficiently lacking in both intimacy and grandeur to be the "home from home" of the rootless and cultureless families who inhabit it for the season. Its vast public rooms with their gilded decoration but scanty furniture, its supper eaten at a long common table, all suggest, especially in view of America's lead in the modern design of hotels, a very primitive stage in evolution toward even the Stentorian of *The Custom of the Country.* The boarders are rich stock-broking and real-estate-dealing characters who have bought New York houses, if sometimes inadvertently in the wrong area, with the wives and daughters who have failed to gain admittance to the much simpler houses of the old upper class. One would not describe them as having "a mannered lack of manners," to use again the phrase coined by Richard Chase; they live in a more primordial state of anarchy. It is presumably not their fault that there are not enough young men to go round at dances, but the races, for example, are usually not a smartly social and, as James would say, "bisexual" occasion, but a rather sordid spree for husbands while the wives sit idly at the hotel, dressed in the height of fashion. The simple gastronomic advantage, let alone the courtesy, of punctuality for the communal meals has not been perceived—this last failure in routine as a symbol of breakdown forms a significant little cross-reference between novels. If the habits of the Saratoga families are presented as having, according to traditional conventions, distinctly plebeian features, their way of thinking and feeling is as undemocratic as it is vulgar; snobbery in terms of an objection to someone else's "edging up" to one indicates both qualities.

Three families emerge from the undifferentiated crowd: the Elmsworths, who are old *habitués* but less prosperous than they were, the St. Georges, who are very decidedly—and a little recklessly—on the ascent, and the Clossons, who are engaged in getting themselves accepted by the others. Mrs. St. George is admirably calculated to be at first the representative consciousness of the group. She combines a slight technical uncertainty at the table and a deeper sense of social inferiority with an equally powerful sense of superiority toward the Clossons, Mrs. Closson being a Brazilian divorcée of peculiarly unorthodox personal habits. However, her husband's business exigencies force a rapprochement with the Clossons and the following conversation sums up the clash of snobbish with plain vulgarity:

> "If you think I'm going to let my making a big rake-off depend on whether the Clossons had a parson to tie the knot, or only the town-clerk . . ."
> "I've got girls to think of," his wife faltered.
> "It's the girls I'm thinking of, too. D'you suppose I'd sweat and slave down town the way I do if it wasn't for the girls?"
> "But I've got to think of the girls they go with, if they're to marry nice young men."
> "The nice young men'll show up in larger numbers if I can put this deal through. And what's the matter with the Closson girl? She's as pretty as a picture." [Edith Wharton, *The Buccaneers*, D. Appleton & Co., Bk. I, 3. Copyright 1938 Edith Wharton. Quoted by permission.]

The Clossons are peculiar in other ways. Conchita is normally a Spanish name; de Santos Dios is, in so far as it is anything, incorrect Spanish; and the young man appears to sing a Spanish song. Surely Edith Wharton in her old age cannot really have been getting as vague as the Marchioness of Brightlingsea is later shown to be (she thinks the language of Brazil is, or was, Spanish)? Jacqueline March, who is supposed to be knowledgeable, is also made unaware not only that Brazil was once part of the Portuguese Empire, but that it was still an empire in its own right at the time of the novel. Such carelessness with detail—this is not the first reference to Brazil in Edith Wharton's work—does not affect the main themes or the broad handling of the story, but it can only be called a sign of weakening powers.[1] It is odd that Lapsley also apparently did not notice it.

The ill-assorted group of families who have no traditions to look back on, no current forms and manners to guide them in the present, but plenty of money and vigorous impulses toward worldly advancement, seem indeed the "first-born of chaos." Social ambition, which is of course a sense of purpose, ironically considered, distinguishes them from the millionaires in *The Children*, who desire only idleness, and the American female section at least has strict sexual morals; but Edith Wharton has probably cut her families off from the Puritan tradition as completely as can be imagined in the circumstances. Out of the group there emerges the vision of the modern buccaneers.

> Ah, but there they were, the girls!—the privileged few whom she grouped under that designation. The fancy had taken them to come in late, and to arrive all together; and now, arm-in-arm, a blushing bevy, they swayed across the threshold of the dining-room like a branch hung with blos-

1. There had been one or two little anachronistic lapses, references to Vernon Lee and Paul Bourget, in *The Age of Innocence*. See Introduction to the edition of 1953, London: Lehman.

soms, drawing the dull middle-aged eyes of the other guests from lobster salad and fried chicken, and eclipsing even the refulgent colonel—happy girls, with two new dancers for the week-end, they had celebrated the unwonted wind-fall by extra touches of adornment: a red rose in the fold of a fichu, a loose curl on a white shoulder, a pair of new satin slippers, a fresh *moiré* ribbon.

Seeing them through the eyes of the new young men Mrs. St. George felt their collective grace with a vividness almost exempt from envy. To her, as to those two foreigners they embodied "the American girl," the world's highest achievement; and she was as ready to enjoy Lizzie Elmsworth's brilliant darkness, and that dry sparkle of Mab's, as much as her own Virginia's roses, and Nan's alternating frowns and dimples. She was even able to recognize that the Closson girl's incongruous hair gilded the whole group like a sun-burst. Could Newport show anything lovelier . . . ? [*The Buccaneers,* Bk. I, 3. Quoted by permission.]

We are invited to share Mrs. St. George's feelings, but the passage is, nevertheless, saved from mere sentimentality by the humor of the description, by the reference to their characteristic unpunctuality, and by what we know about their various other foibles. By at first investing the idea with Mrs. St. George's own absurdity, the author is, as it were, issuing a challenge to herself to validate it as a serious theme by further developments. During the rest of Book I attention is concentrated more and more on Nan and on the governess whom her mother's muddled ambition has provided, Laura Testvalley.

Laura Testvalley is, all reservations having been made, one of Edith Wharton's great creations. Her family background links her to major aspects of European life and art, while in herself she is a connoisseur of social types and ways of life. She has seen English aristocratic life on the highest level, and from the inside, in all its meanness and dreariness as well as splendor—we later learn that she has had a clandestine affair with a cretinous younger son. With characteristic determination she has decided, in order to keep her distinguished but destitute relations, to come where she can earn a higher salary and, furthermore, to go beyond the limits of New York Society, which she naturally finds tame. In short, she is a free intelligence and, in her undemonstrative way, an independent woman of the world in a wholly complimentary sense, without fixed class associations and able to establish herself anywhere on her own terms. We are invited to admire the poise with which she treats her former lover rather than to censure the lapse of the past. The charming scene of her arrival shows that she can cope with any situation. It is only during this stage that we are told that she is small and brown; her personality makes the first impact on us as well as on the girls and their parents. She is shown adapting herself rapidly to circumstances, though her own experiences, indicated in a superb reminiscent section, and what she sees happening around her make her uneasy about the freedom of social intercourse at all hours among American youth. It is she who contrives to get the older girls into New York Society and ultimately to link the Saratoga provincials to the Society of two continents. The hasty marriage of Lord Richard Marable and Conchita Closson brings out another provinciality, the farcical ignorance of the rest of the world on the part of the British aristocracy. However, his mother, Lady Brightlingsea's cable, "Is she black?" is nicely balanced against Mrs. Closson's question, "I don't suppose the Marquess is in business, is he?" One has here the beginning of a pattern of two-way irony, which is to develop and deepen as the book proceeds. Already one sees suggested a preliminary and approximate "placing" of the newly rich, the old New York upper class—Laura Testvalley has worked for a Mrs. Parmore—and the British nobility. Laura Testvalley is at present in the center, a confidante of everyone and the arbiter of social destiny. In the meanwhile, however, Nan St. George is being established alongside her, so that her mother's vision can become a reality for the critical reader. Although it is some time before she is made the center of consciousness, she has already been made to stand out above the rest of her associates. Though only sixteen, she has both perceptiveness and intelligence, which are shown in her witty mimicry of her mother. Childish weaknesses are balanced by her capacity for seeing her mistakes and her delicacy in making amends. Nan never loses her independent identity and fresh impulsiveness of speech and opinion. Book I has one or two less finished passages but forms a remarkably vivid presentation of a crude, formless and undirected, yet aspiring and overflowing, society.

Book II opens with a full effect of contrast in a Mayfair at the height of its glory and where the buccaneers have already established a foothold. The new situation is first shown to us with greater subtlety by using the eyes of a compatriot, Miss Jacqueline March, herself an earlier "marauder," as she puts it, who now lives vicariously on her aristocratic connections; her whole situation is dramatized with multiple irony. Her understanding of upper-class England and of her own life, and the author's understanding of both, are concentrated in her vision of the tired but still magnificent warhorse, the Marchioness of Brightlingsea:

> Slowly she drew herself up from the sofa-corner. She was so tall that the ostrich plumes on her bonnet might have brushed Miss March's ceiling had they not drooped instead of towering. Miss March had often wondered how her friend managed to have such an air of majesty when everything about her flopped and dangled. "Ah—it's their secret," she thought, and rejoiced that at least she could recognize and admire the attribute in her noble English friends. So many of her travelling compatriots seemed not to understand, or even to perceive, the difference. They were the ones who could not see what she "got out" of her little London house, and her little London life. [*The Buccaneers*, Bk. II, 8. Quoted by permission.]

If she has not struck roots, Jacqueline March has grafted herself on to English Society, whereas Laura Testvalley is a free agent. The scene is made a prelude to, and her biography a parody of, what is to follow. After reading *Madame de Treymes,* Henry James had advised Edith Wharton to write about English life, but, apart from a few short stories, she had not previously attempted it. Her knowledge of French upper-class life had been acquired early and was profound, but, despite her frequent visits to England before the First World War and her close friendship with James and Howard Sturgis, she did not formulate her impressions till the thirties, when she wrote her amusing chapter in *A Backward Glance* in which she recalls the "passing amusement from such fugitive dips into a foreign society." She obviously found the London "crushes" and formal dinners too reminiscent in cultural dimness of the New York parties of her earlier married life; one or two anecdotes correspond closely. In *The Buccaneers* one finds a picture of English county and aristocratic life, more panoramic than the French picture in *The Custom of the Country,* and more penetrating in its interpretation, while the thematic contrasts with America stand out superbly. We are given studies of two families at the top of the hierarchy and of a family of squires characteristically more ancient than either. Attachment to place, devotion to duties of family and community, subjection to social form, indifference to physical discomfort and sacrifice of personal convenience, and even of happiness, are the well-known common qualities. They are shown with their accompanying fantastic arrogance, frequent absurdity, and breath-taking hypocrisy. The earlier chapters of Lady Diana Cooper's autobiography provide some amusing parallels. The three families exemplify variations impossible to the Americans; indeed Edith Wharton has adapted to her purpose something of the "mad milord" tradition. Out of the international merger new lines of thought and conduct begin, as has been said, to take shape.

We start in chronological order with the Thwartes of Honourslove in the Cotswolds:

> In the long summer twilight a father and son were pacing the terrace of an old house called Honourslove, on the edge of the Cotswold. The irregular silver-gray building, when approached from the village by a drive winding under ancient beech-trees, seemed, like so many old dwellings in England, to lie almost in a hollow, screened to the north by hanging woods, and surveying from its many windows only its own lawns and trees; but the terrace on the other front overlooked an immensity of hill and vale, with huddled village roofs and floating spires. Now, in the twilight, though the sky curved above so clear and luminous, everything below was blurred, and the spires were hardly distinguishable from the tree-trunks; but to the two men strolling up and down before the house long familiarity made every fold of the landscape visible. . . .
>
> . . . the young respect nothing and believe in nothing, least of all in the validity of tradition. Guy did, however believe in Honourslove, the beautiful old place which had come to be the first and last article of the family creed. Tradition, as embodied in the ancient walls and the ancient trees of Honourslove, seemed to him as priceless a quality as it did to Sir Helmsley; and indeed he sometimes said to himself that if ever he succeeded to the baronetcy he would be a safer and more vigilant guardian than his father, who loved the place and yet had so often betrayed it. [*The Buccaneers*, Bk. II, 9. Quoted by permission.]

It is a vision of the English manor-house with all its traditional associations, offered unashamedly for simple acceptance. Sir Helmsley has aspired to be

> the model landowner, crack shot, leader and champion in all traditionally British pursuits and pleasures; but a contrary streak in his nature was perpetually driving him toward art and poetry and travel, odd intimacies with a group of painters and decorators of socialistic tendencies, reckless dalliance with ladies, and a loud contempt for the mental inferiority of his

county neighbours. [*The Buccaneers,* Bk. II, 9. Quoted by permission.]

Guy, on the other hand, is an unqualified value from the first; he combines devotion to tradition and "point to point" riding with personal charm and adaptability to the present and the future. He has become a railway engineer in order to make a fortune abroad and save the house from the estate market. No unprejudiced reader could do otherwise than accept him at the author's valuation and await developments.

We are shown the next house as it appears to the Americans, with significant irony and another significant pointer to Nan's preeminence above the rest:

> The St. George girls had never seen anything as big as the house at Allfriars except a public building, and as they drove toward it down the long avenue, and had their first glimpse of Inigo Jones's most triumphant expression of the Palladian dream, Virginia said with a little shiver: "Mercy—it's just like a gaol."
> "Oh, no—a palace," Nan corrected.
> Virginia gave an impatient laugh. "I'd like to know where you've ever seen a palace."
> "Why, hundreds of times, I have, in my dreams."
> "You mustn't tell your dreams. Miss Testvalley says nothing bores people so much as being told other people's dreams."
> Nan said nothing, but an iron gate seemed to clang shut in her; the gate that was so often slammed by careless hands. As if any one could be bored by such dreams as hers! [*The Buccaneers,* Bk. II, 10. Quoted by permission.]

Allfriars is the seat of the Marquess of Brightlingsea and Edith Wharton makes it an example of another aspect of the tradition. It is a vision of dilapidated splendor, to the upkeep of which all the family resources are devoted, though no one has in fact any aesthetic appreciation of it. We have in these scenes the sheer emptiness of aristocratic life, uncomprehending care of property, and the weary performance of a routine which, if it still has a remnant of meaning, has lost all glamor or vitality. The Marquess is a caricature of the great nobleman. Nevertheless Nan is moved by the beauty of the place and for the first time her sensitivity to the "murmur of the past" becomes an explicit theme. This is taken up immediately in a return to Honourslove, with all the contrasts stated and implied:

> After the shabby vastness of Allfriars everything about Honourslove seemed to Nan St. George warm, cared-for, exquisitely intimate. The stones of the house, the bricks of the walls, the very flags of the terrace, were so full of captured sunshine that in the darkest days they must keep an inner brightness. Nan, though too ignorant to single out the details of all this beauty, found herself suddenly at ease with the soft mellow place, as though some secret thread of destiny attached her to it.
>
> Guy Thwarte, somewhat to her surprise, had kept at her side during the walk and the visit to the chapel. He had not said much, but with him also Nan had felt instantly at ease. In his answers to her questions she had detected a latent passion for every tree and stone of the beautiful old place—a sentiment new to her experience, as a dweller in houses without histories, but exquisitely familiar to her imagination. . . .
>
> "You see now why I wanted you to come to Honourslove," he said in an odd new voice.
>
> She was still looking at him thoughtfully. "You knew I'd understand."
>
> "Oh, everything!"
>
> She sighed for pleasure; but then: "No. There's one thing I don't understand. How you can go away and leave it all for so long."
>
> He gave a nervous laugh. "You don't know England. That's part of our sense of beyondness: I'd do more than that for those old stones." [*The Buccaneers*, Bk. II, 11. Quoted by permission.]

One feels, and it is surprising in Edith Wharton, that the idiom of the last clause is not quite cis-Atlantic. The sentiment is, however, genuinely English and in the scene as a whole an extremely important stage in the unfolding of Nan's character is also dramatized. Her distinction is shown in her development's being as much a realization of potentialities as a response to experience. The future in all its implications is now skilfully and unobtrusively foreshadowed in the final tableau:

> . . . for a long while they stood side by side without speaking, each seeing the other in every line of the landscape. [*The Buccaneers*, Bk. II, 11. Quoted by permission.]

Nan St. George's response to the English scene is far more than superior tourism; it is part of a new approach to life that becomes clearer as the story continues. The others are as ill at ease with history and traditions as they are with the maids Laura Testvalley provides to wait on them.

After living tradition and moribund ritual, Edith Wharton provides an episode of English upper-class informality in "a bungalow" on the Thames at Runnymede belonging to Lady Churt, who represents "fast" Society, the Marlborough House set. It is made an English counterpart of Saratoga, with all the differences implied, but the daughters entertain eligible young men with a combination of American freedom and American respectability under the careful stage management of Laura Testvalley and Jacky March, representing intrigue and decorum respectively. The invasion, as the former calls it, is moving faster than the comparable invasion of old New York that begins *The Custom of the Country*, but it is in any case more of an exchange of advantages than a mere annexation. The Americans have found that England has something to offer that survives their conquest, even though they do not quite understand, as Miss March says, "what a duke is." Edith Wharton now separates Nan from the others and appropriately focuses our attention on the Duke of Tintagel.

As with the Brightlingseas and Seadown, or "Seedy," their heir, she once again shows as nice a sense of English territorial nomenclature as she does elsewhere with the family names of her native New York. The Duke is known as Ushant, his original courtesy title, and is her third

specimen of aristocratic oddity and the center of another
variation on the English social order, the fundamentally
"little" man overawed by his own inherited position but
conscientiously and actively believing in it and anxious
to do his duty to the utmost:

> He meant, if possible, to keep up in suitable state both
> Tintagel and Longlands, as well as Folyat House, his London
> residence; but he meant to do so without the continual drain
> on his fortune which his father had been obliged to incur.
> The new Duke hoped that, by devoting all his time and most
> of his faculties to the care of his estates and the personal su-
> pervision of his budget, he could reduce his cost of living
> without altering its style; and the indefatigable Duchess, her
> numerous daughters notwithstanding, found time to second
> the attempt. She was not the woman to let her son forget the
> importance of her aid; and though a perfect understanding
> had always reigned between them, recent symptoms made it
> appear that the young Duke was beginning to chafe under
> her regency. [*The Buccaneers,* Bk. II, 14. Quoted by permis-
> sion.]

As he insists that he will only marry a girl "who doesn't
know what a duke is," interest in the buccaneers is inevitable, but one does not feel embarrassed by a sense of
contrivance. The convergence of himself and Nan in a
seafog among the ruins of the original castle is in fact
a revealing piece of comedy. Her simplicity and her failure
to recognize him—they have met before at Runnymede—
produce in him a blend of injured vanity and security
that satisfies him, and is a delight to the reader's ironical
contemplation. To her he is now "one of the stupidest
young men [she has] ever met," which indicates, if nothing
else, her independence and her lack of respect for mere
persons. The big later scene at Runnymede that leads up
to the conclusions of the invasion has been rightly admired. Edith Wharton brings about her alliances by a
brilliant playing off of national characteristics. The opening conversation, in which the younger Elmsworth girl

challenges Hector Robinson, the representative of the
English industrial and political world, about Lord Seadown's intentions toward her sister, makes a more than
usually strong contrast in manners, besides emphasizing
that the latter's procrastination has given scope for rivalry
among the hunters of coronets and to a new propected alliance. The final irony is a demonstration by Lady Churt
that her class can, in a sense, deal with any situation, but
her actual defeat symbolizes a victory for, and endorsement
of, American values of sincerity, honesty, and free-speak-
ing, despite any incidental brashness or predatoriness, over
aristocratic corruption and sophistication.

The remainder of Book II is on the ducal level. The
Duke of Tintagel's call on Miss Testvalley, which begins
with an inspection of a clock—his one hobby is orology—
and ends with a very detached and businesslike enquiry
about his prospects of acceptance by Nan, is excellent
comedy of a quieter kind, and his desire for an unsophisticated bride is a straight half-and-half mixture of defensive
aud dominating egotism. Edith Wharton puts her summing up of the Anglo-American *entente* into the form of
a letter from Sir Helmsley Thwarte to his son now in
Brazil. As an intellectual as well as a squire, he can, just
plausibly and with certain amusing overtones of irony,
be made to see both the value of "our Dukery . . . in sub-
versive times like these" and "the unheard-of and incom-
prehensible phenomenon that a great English country-seat
offers to the unprejudiced gaze of the American back-
woodsman and his females." As we have seen, both the
traditions and the representatives of English Society are
subjected to a searching scrutiny. The values stand after
the demolition of absurdities and falsities, and the American contribution is treated as a revitalization. With all the
reverence shown for old New York traditions in earlier
novels, none of its representatives is presented to us as
having such actual vigor and potentialities of achievement

as Guy Thwarte; on the other hand every possibility in Nan St. George is also, as Sir Helmsley says, "engaging." The next stage of the plot is now prepared for; the American parents are increasingly out of their depth and about to disappear, and the buccaneers are becoming naturalized.

Book III opens after another two-year gap with a vision of the social triumph of the invasion; Nan St. George, now Duchess of Tintagel, is at her desk in the Correggio Room of Longlands, the original ducal seat. The "American girl" is busy with her new duties; symbolically, she is coping with the social correspondence, which involves an exact knowledge of the hierarchical system at the top of which she is placed. Whereas the other American girls are so intellectually and emotionally shallow that, after an initial shock, greater than hers at the time, they have fitted themselves into English Society, Nan, being intelligent and sensitive, is still bewildered both by refinements of social and domestic organization and the impropriety (as she feels her mother-in-law ought to see it if she were really to look) of the great pictures. The Duke is beginning to learn that, as his mother puts it, "women are not quite as simple as clocks" and, as to Nan, her old associates find that, though exalted above them all, she is "unfashionable among the unfashionable." But it is a further irony that, though the Duke is as unsocial as she is, this never becomes a bond of sympathy; a fixed and a free mind cannot understand each other. Hers is now the point of view, and we are given, mainly as she sees it, the background of her present predicament. It becomes apparent that she has married, not for a title, but for history:

> She did not admit to herself that her first sight of the ruins of the ancient Tintagel had played a large part in her wooing; that if the Duke had been only the dullest among the amiable but dull young men who came to the bungalow at Runnymede she would hardly have given him a second thought. But the idea of living in that magic castle by the

sad western sea had secretly tinged her vision of the castle's owner. [*The Buccaneers*, Bk. III, 20. Quoted by permission.]

Her husband, however, has no interest in the "rich low murmur of the past," as the phrase comes this time, but an active concern with present economic problems and responsibilities that he is determined to share with no one. His painstakingly but detachedly benevolent despotism is pitted against her rather muddle-headed but more human kindness in a battle of wills over a village typhoid case, and the conflict is dramatized in hysterical rebellion, a miscarriage, and a nervous breakdown. One's only comment is that it is extraordinary that anyone as knowledgeable as Edith Wharton should talk of drains of any kind in connection with a cottage in 19th-century rural Cornwall! Annabel's tragic situation is clear to her:

> She had understood it without being told, she had acknowledged it and wept over it at the time; but the irremediable had been done, and she knew that never, in her husband's eyes, would any evidence of repentance atone for that night's disaster. [*The Buccaneers*, Bk. III, 20. Quoted by permission.]

She feels herself out of touch with both her own past and the present in which she does not understand her role. The sensitive and independent girl is becoming a lively and thoughtful woman who cannot conform to any social pattern unless she understands it and believes in it. It is apparent that, even by her isolation and her diagnosis of her own circumstances, Annabel is now a character of considerable interest and distinction.

The situation is complicated emotionally, but brought nearer clarification in terms of thematic development, by the reappearance of Guy Thwarte after an eventful sojourn in Brazil. He also is a different person but

> As he stood there, looking out over the bare November landscape, and the soft blue hills fading into a low sky, the sense

of kinship between himself and the soil began to creep through him once more. [*The Buccaneers,* Bk. III, 21. Quoted by permission.]

The climax of Book III is the Christmas house-party at Longlands, the big exemplification of Anglo-American mixed manners, and the climax of the party is the dialogue between Annabel and Guy; she first confesses—and it is appropriate that she confesses to him:

"But I've tried this—and I sometimes think I wasn't meant for it. . . ." She broke off, and he saw the tears in her eyes.

"My dear child—" he began; and then, half-embarrassed: "For you *are* a child still, you know. Have you any idea how awfully young you are?"

As soon as he had spoken he reflected that she was too young not to resent any allusion to her inexperience. She laughed. "Please don't send me back to the nursery! 'Little girls shouldn't ask questions. You'll understand better when you're grown up' . . . How much longer am I to be talked to like that?"

"I'm afraid that's the most troublesome question of all. The truth is—" he hesitated. "I rather think growing up's largely a question of climate—of sunshine . . . Perhaps our moral climate's too chilly for you young creatures from across the globe. After all, New York's in the latitude of Naples."

She gave him a perplexed look, and then smiled. "Oh, I know those burning hot summers. . . ."

"You want so much to go back to them?"

"Do I? I can't tell. . . . I don't believe so. . . . But somehow it seems as if this were wrong—my being here. . . . If you knew what I'd give to be able to try again . . . somewhere where I could be myself, you understand, not just an unsuccessful Duchess." [*The Buccaneers,* Bk. III, 22. Quoted by permission.]

Her intelligence and personal poise give the lie to his sympathetic but unintentionally patronizing attitude, and the post-mortem scene with the Dowager is a straight confrontation of two social points of view, or rather of a mere honest individual and a whole system. To the Dowager's pronouncement:

> "Duchesses, you know, are like soldiers; they must often be under arms while others are amusing themselves."

Annabel replies:

> "I think I'm tired of trying to be English. . . . I think it might be better if I left him; then he could marry somebody else, and have a lot of children. Wouldn't that be best?" [*The Buccaneers,* Bk. III, 23. Quoted by permission.]

The Dowager's conduct of the scene exemplifies all the virtues of her class and of her principles, and the conclusion is highly significant:

> "The gong, my dear! You must not keep your guests waiting. . . . I'll follow you at once. . . ."
> ". . . Her heart was beating high after the agitation of her talk with her mother-in-law, but as she descended the wide shallow steps of the great staircase (up and down which it would have been a profanation to gallop, as one used to up and down the steep narrow stairs at home) she reflected that the Dowager, though extremely angry, and even scandalized, had instantly put an end to their discussion when she heard the summons to luncheon. Annabel remembered the endless wordy wrangles between her mother, her sister and herself, and thought how little heed they would have paid to a luncheon-gong in the thick of one of their daily disputes. Here it was different: everything was done by rule, and according to tradition, and for the Duchess of Tintagel to keep her guests waiting for luncheon would have been an offence against the conventions almost as great as that of not being at her post when the company were leaving the night before. A year ago Annabel would have laughed at these rules and observances: now, though they chafed her no less, she was beginning to see the use of having one's whims and one's rages submitted to some kind of control. "It did no good to anybody to have us come down with red noses to a stone-cold lunch, and go upstairs afterward to sulk in our bedrooms," she thought, and she recalled how her father, when regaled

with the history of these domestic disagreements, used to say with a laugh: "What a lot of nonsense it would knock out of you women to have to hoe a potato-field, or spend a week in Wall Street."

Yes, in spite of her anger, in spite of her desperate sense of being trapped, Annabel felt in a confused way that the business of living was perhaps conducted more wisely at Longlands—even though Longlands was the potato-field she was destined to hoe for life. [*The Buccaneers,* Bk. III, 23. Quoted by permission.]

There are several layers of irony, a criticism of ducal etiquette, a criticism of Annabel also and a comparison, itself full of implications, of etiquette to a simple daily task. Here one has the social theme embodied in the character and consciousness of Annabel in a particular situation; she appreciates the dignity and amenity of the left she loathes. It is the most telling recurrence of the symbol of the fixed mealtime.

The rest of the novel is concerned with working out the implications of the mature standpoint she has reached; she is poised between two worlds and able to contemplate and evaluate, despite her unhappy personal involvement, the merits and defects of both. There are certain gaps, and the last three chapters, as we have them, are decidedly sketchy, but it is difficult to believe that, as Gaillard Lapsley suggests in his note at the end, the Elmsworth girls would have been given a fuller treatment now or earlier, unless this could have been managed without deflecting the focus from Annabel. The complexity of the situation is not disentangled at once, however, and one does not imagine that it would ever have become simple. The other buccaneers have merely fitted into their looser and faster version of English Society, and they accept its formalities and financial stringencies for the sake of the public glamor and private excitement. Annabel has a more significant destiny. She and Guy Thwarte are being gradually brought together on a basis of her need for his support and his realization of how he must behave toward her, now her maturity is complete. Here the text begins to peter out, but we know from the plan that there was to have been a sensational elopement, aided by Laura Testvalley, and that Annabel and Guy were to have married for "deep and abiding love." Annabel is still partly marrying for history, but this time in the person of a fine-looking, intelligent, energetic, and charming young man. Her motives have already been summarized before the possibility of achievement became clear:

> . . . Life in England had a background, layers and layers of rich deep background, of history, poetry, old traditional observances, beautiful houses, beautiful landscapes, beautiful ancient buildings, palaces, churches, cathedrals. Would it not be possible, in some mysterious way, to create for one's self a life out of all this richness . . . ? [*The Buccaneers,* Bk. III, 24. Quoted by permission.]

There is no doubt that she has come to dominate the scene. Her repudiation of social anarchy and acceptance of the idea of order—if not the order of the Tintagel household—with all the feeling for its necessary setting in time and place, together with her personal simplicity and independence, make her a very remarkable character indeed and her union with Guy Thwarte, who stands for all the ancient obligations and courtesies of his class, combined with a new managerial efficiency, as we should put it today, suggests a prototype of moral and social revolution working itself out in individual lives toward a stable balance of old and new, a reunion of two worlds based on mutual understanding and a foundation for the future. This would seem to be the "criticism of life" embodied in *The Buccaneers,* and its relationship to Edith Wharton's previous work. One presumes that the visit to South Africa referred to at the end of the plan represents a new engineering contract and, in the circumstances, a discreet temporary withdrawal into the wilderness; the idea of Guy Thwarte and Nan as white settlers would make nonsense of the themes, which have, in every case and despite the then well-nigh insuperable difficulties in the position of an ex-duchess, pointed toward a new start in the old setting.

Looked at historically, this could, of course, have been only an attempt at an individual solution of the problem, and Edith Wharton would not have been exemplifying a general trend. Neither Society nor the community around it changed very much in England in the 19th century; Howard Sturgis's picture of the turn of the century in *Belchamber* is substantially the same as Edith Wharton's. However, Victoria Sackville-West's delightful interpretation of high life, as seen from the inside above—and below —stairs, in *The Edwardians,* ends with her young Duke in a rather different situation from Guy Thwarte's. The manners and morals, especially the morals, of Society have relaxed a good deal, although the outward shell still stands —divorce is still unthinkable for the aristocracy—but possibilities of change are being freely discussed and, as regards the wider social relationships, it is now a matter not merely of preservation but of adaptation of his inheritance in order to remain part of a more rapidly changing community. Pursuit of the comparison further would become too hypothetical. One may perhaps end by saying that Edith Wharton's study of the search for order and harmony and a satisfying relationship to environment in an individual life must surely keep its relevance and interest in any community. It is scarcely possible to imagine human conditions in which conflict between groups and between generations, and the falsity or genuineness of their claims and aspirations, are not fundamental problems of social morality. These themes form the inner life and energizing spirit of the novel.

11 *Concluding Observations*

In drawing together these impressions of Edith Wharton's work, one must tackle first its relationship to that of James. Influence and discipleship have probably been exaggerated, but they are undoubtedly a feature and one that does not need to be either praised or deprecated. She tells us of her immense admiration for James's work at the start of her literary career, and its manifestations in her early stories and *nouvelles* is pretty plain. As has been shown, it is a matter of stylistic polish and formality and closely organized construction in the treatment of social and moral themes; having regard to dates, the resemblance between *The Pelican* and *Greville Fane*, between the situations of the eloquent but unqualified lecturer and the fluent but uninspired novelist, could be a limited piece or plagiarism or may be merely an interesting parallel. There can be no doubt that *Madame de Treymes* derives its central situation from *The American*. The less pointed contrasts and the subtler realism of Edith Wharton's novel show her originality, but one could not, of course, take this *nouvelle* by itself as evidence of her superiority as a novelist. We are not in any case concerned with a crude issue of superiority and inferiority, but rather with aesthetic differences and personal qualities. Edith Wharton's distinctive characteristics are her far stronger sense of the ramifications of social class and of the tension between the individual and the group, and her capacity for seeing a human situation in close and significant relation to its material setting. These are characteristics that invite comparison with Balzac or with George Eliot rather than with James, and her own adverse criticism of the later James[1] for suspending his characters in the void is worth recalling. The other novel that harks back to James is of course *The Age of Innocence*. In this case one finds, on the one hand, the characteristically rich period setting and penetrating sociological observation, in a word, a fuller realism than in *The Europeans*, but, paradoxically, less poise and subtlety in the treatment of themes than in James's more schematic tale. On the whole, Edith Wharton's literary relationship to James seems of an ordinary kind: a general debt to him as a source of inspiration and technique, one or two particular borrowings, and, beyond this, the deployment of a comparable, but lesser and also very different, genius.

One can, however, profitably carry comparison a good deal further in certain directions. Other novels can be compared in certain respects and there is the larger topic of their treatment of the American scene. We know how deeply conscious James was from an early age of "the complex fate of being an American" and of his relationship to his "native land." The famous passages in *Hawthorne* and later *The American Scene* may seem a little sentimental and even absurd amid the *sansculotterie* of the present day, but the first three volumes of Leon Edel's *Life* make James's position and its background clear, and James's own note of 1881 clinches the matter with wonderful insight—and foresight:

> My choice is the old world—my choice, my need, my life . . .
> . . . My impressions here are exactly what I expected they would be, and I scarcely see the place, and feel the manners, the race, the tone of things, now that I am on the spot, more vividly than I did while I was still in Europe. My work lies there—and with this vast new world, *je n'ai que faire*. One

---

1. See Chapter 9 above.

can't do both—one must choose. No European writer is called upon to assume that terrible burden, and it seems hard that I should be. The burden is necessarily greater for an American—for he must deal, more or less, even if only by implication, with Europe; whereas no European is obliged to deal in the least with America. No one dreams of calling him less complete for not doing so. . . . The painter of manners who neglects America is not thereby incomplete as yet; but a hundred years hence—fifty years hence perhaps—he will doubtless be accounted so.[2]

Beginning about twenty years later, Edith Wharton did in fact deal mainly with an American social scene. She did not, of course, deal with quite the kind of scenes that Howells[3] had thought should be dealt with or that her own younger contemporaries present to us, but she does dramatize a complex and fluid social situation, peculiar to America, if confined in its localization. She shows us a life and manners of fascinating variety and deep moral significance where James saw only a vague "*grope* of wealth" with nowhere to go "on" to. Her reaction to what she knew of American life in the 20s and to the demands for realism of that time bears a superficial resemblance to his reactions to the Boston he visited in the 80s and to its past, but where he felt restricted by a narrow, if sometimes "exquisite," provincialism, she feared that civilization might be lost in a vast, crude, and dreary standardization. Their common attitudes are their hatred of the "middling" and their feeling for fineness, dignity, and intelligence, wherever they may be found. Their modes of expression could never, except perhaps in her early productions, be mistaken for each other's.

Edith Wharton's form and style underwent a very visible evolutionary process during her forty-odd years of creative

2. *The Notebooks of Henry James*, ed. F. O. Matthiessen and K. B. Murdock, New York: Oxford University Press, 1947, pp. 23–24.
3. For example, in his review of James's *Hawthorne* in *The Atlantic Monthly*, February, 1880.

effort. Her principles, as set out in *The Writing of Fiction* and other critical writings, are fairly exemplified in her novels and stories before that date. Her two great books, *The House of Mirth* and *The Custom of the Country,* and the New England stories are, as has been shown, closely written and compactly organized, as carefully planned as *The Golden Bowl* or *The Ambassadors* and yet packed with life, so that the novels especially have that double quality of formal economy and the apparent tendency "to burst, with a latent extravagance [their] mould."[4] One need not expatiate again on their human depth and breadth. The inferior novels of the early 20s are well made; the quality Edith Wharton calls "stylization" is maintained, but as, presumably, she began to feel that "verisimilitude" demanded a relaxation of old "conventions," she began to relax the structural order of her work. The double plot of *The Children* makes possible an even freer interplay of attitudes and behavior than one finds in the more complex prewar novels, so different from this and from each other—*The Fruit of the Tree* and *The Custom of the Country.* The career of Vance Weston spreads itself through a veritable "loose and baggy monster" in two parts; the episodes are significant as experience for the hero, but only in a very general way in relation to each other. One does not make any great claims for these two novels, but in *The Buccaneers* juxtapositions are made to represent the clash of cultures, and the varieties of social experience demand a frequently changing scene. Furthermore, in this last work Edith Wharton broke triumphantly with her own basic principle, that the tale should "work itself out from not more than two (or at most three) angles of vision";[5] she changes the angle frequently until the heroine is ready to assume command of the whole situation. Here one may see how, despite certain vicissi-

---

4. James's phrase from the Preface to *The Portrait of a Lady.*
5. *The Writing of Fiction,* p. 87.

tudes, Edith Wharton maintained her creative powers and freedom of approach to her material to the last.

The loosening texture, but by no means disintegration, of Edith Wharton's style has been mentioned already as each stage of her career has been discussed. It is perhaps worth making a further point about her dialogue. Recent critics have impugned its authenticity as a representation, however stylized, of American speech. This is a point on which the foreigner can seldom speak with conviction, but one feels compelled to draw attention to the opinions of E. K. Brown and R. M. Lovett[6] that she had a flair for naturalistic dialogue. Adverse criticism has been of more recent date[7] and its authors may themselves have forgotten the flavor of the 20s; was not New York conversation perhaps fuller of Anglicisms then, as London conversation is of Americanisms now?[8] Nothing sounds sillier than the silliness of an earlier decade, which was what Edith Wharton was recording satirically.

Edith Wharton wrote forty-six books between her thirty-fifth year and her death at the age of seventy-five. It is a formidable achievement for a well-to-do Society woman, comparable in bulk to that of James and surpassing that of most professional writers in English. One does not claim greatness for her on a quantitative basis, but one cannot and should not altogether ignore it. If one tries to look without prejudice at the American novel, it seems less a question of whom to place her with than of whom one is to place along with her in a class just below that of James, of the great but not supremely great. Of the novelists of man in modern society no one would now rate Howells very high, despite his intentions. Norris, Dreiser, and

---

6. Brown, Chapter XII, and Lovett, p. 70.
7. For example in Van Wyck Brooks, *The Confident Years,* Chapter XVI.
8. H. L. Mencken is inconclusive on this topic in his chapter on "American and English" in *The American Language,* 4th edition, New York: Knopf, 1936.

Lewis, Edith Wharton's younger contemporaries, are remarkable, but their vitality is crude and their values of enterprise and frankness are, however admirable, paradoxically limited. Though they wrote about a wide new world that she did not know, they do not merely reject, they ignore, in their respective visions, the heritage of civilization, and one finds oneself returning, however unfashionably, to James's implied diagnosis that there is a large-scale provinciality as well as a small—"I think it extremely provincial for a Russian to be very Russian. . . ."[9] One feels convinced that Edith Wharton not only made a finer contribution in every way to the art of the novel than any of these writers, but one at least as good as that of any of their successors in any mode. One cannot, however, deny the positive values of the realists, and Mrs. Leavis, in looking[10]—with a characteristic eye for essentials—at Edith Wharton's claim to recognition as a major novelist, finds her lacking in "positives" except for her poor and unsophisticated characters, such as Miss Bunner or Ethan Frome, and consequently feels compelled to place her, despite her intelligence, strength of character, and technical accomplishment, on a lower plane than George Eliot and Jane Austen. One concedes that George Eliot must come first. Edith Wharton's sophistication, though giving her wider scope, almost inevitably makes her more sharply critical of human foibles and more impatient of anti-social behavior. The brilliance of her satire must not, however, dazzle one into exaggerating her negative qualities at the expense of positive enthusiasms and more constructive movements in certain books. Compassion for the unfortunate and a high valuation of toleration and understanding in the community are recurring attitudes. The grace and dignity of Lily Bart belong to the finer side of a social order which, in going rotten, condi-

9. *Letters*, ed. P. Lubbock, 1:12.
10. See "Henry James's Heiress."

tions her downfall. The debilitated standards represented by the Marvells and the more robust, if not entirely attractive, principles represented by Raymond de Chelles nevertheless command our respect. It may be argued that these are in fact more specialized and ephemeral than the basic virtues of the poor. But Edith Wharton was not tied and bound down to the past she was rooted in. Justine Brent is a fine free intelligence though she ends in captivity. Nona Manford represents a new and exploratory moral and social attitude, even though she ends in frustration. One cannot attach as much significance as perhaps one might wish to Vance Weston and Halo Spear, owing to the weaknesses in the artistic realization, but *The Buccaneers* presents us quite clearly with emergent and vital positives and the prospect, despite powerful odds, of a rejuvenated moral and social order in, as it were, prototype. One looks at Edith Wharton again alongside Jane Austen. As, however, one is not concerned with a game of critical musical chairs, one should be content merely to put forward with proper diffidence a claim to comparable status. It is based on six books in particular: *The House of Mirth, The Custom of the Country, Ethan Frome, Summer, Twilight Sleep,* and *The Buccaneers,* and on the evolving pattern of values that manifests itself throughout her work. Edith Wharton made a distinctively upper-class contribution to literature, more distinctively so than James's because she was more concerned with social detail. At the present time, therefore, her work presents something of a challenge to appreciation. It has, however, the body and vigor to support that challenge. Edith Wharton stands for cultural and social continuity and the maintenance, but also the constant readaptation of traditions.

Bibliography

I. Edith Wharton's Works

Books
Almost all were published in both the United States and England in the same year. Only variations are listed.

Verses. Newport: C. E. Hammett, Jr., 1878.
The Decoration of Houses (with Ogden Codman, Jr.). New York: Scribner's, 1897.
The Greater Inclination. New York: Scribner's, 1899.
The Touchstone. New York: Scribner's, 1900. Published in England as *A Gift from the Grave*. London: John Murray, 1900.
Crucial Instances. New York: Scribner's, 1901.
The Valley of Decision. 2 vols. New York: Scribner's, 1902.
Sanctuary. New York: Scribner's, 1903.
The Descent of Man and Other Stories. New York: Scribner's, 1904. Published in England under the same title with the addition of one story, "The Letter." London: Macmillan, 1904.
Italian Villas and Their Gardens. New York: Century, 1904.
Italian Backgrounds. New York: Scribner's, 1905.
The House of Mirth. New York: Scribner's, 1905. World's Classics edition, London: Oxford University Press, 1936, contains the author's Introduction.
Madame de Treymes. New York: Scribner's, 1907.

213

The Fruit of the Tree. New York: Scribner's, 1907.

A Motor-Flight through France. New York: Scribner's, 1908.

The Hermit and the Wild Woman and Other Stories. New York: Scribner's, 1908.

Artemis to Actaeon and Other Verse. New York: Scribner's, 1909.

Tales of Men and Ghosts. New York: Scribner's, 1910.

Ethan Frome. New York: Scribner's, 1911. The Modern Student's Library edition, New York: Scribner's, 1922, contains the author's Introduction.

The Reef. New York: Appleton, 1912.

The Custom of the Country. New York: Scribner's, 1913.

Fighting France, from Dunkerque to Belfort. New York: Scribner's, 1915.

Xingu and Other Stories. New York: Scribner's, 1916.

Summer. New York: Appleton, 1917.

The Marne. New York: Appleton, 1918.

French Ways and Their Meaning. New York: Appleton, 1919.

The Age of Innocence. New York: Appleton, 1920.

In Morocco. New York: Scribner's, 1920.

The Glimpses of the Moon. New York: Appleton, 1922.

A Son at the Front. New York: Scribner's, 1923.

Old New York: False Dawn, The Old Maid, The Spark, New Year's Day. 4 vols. New York: Appleton, 1924.

The Mother's Recompense. New York: Appleton, 1925.

The Writing of Fiction. New York: Scribner's, 1925.

Here and Beyond. New York: Appleton, 1926.

Twelve Poems. London: The Medici Society, 1926.

Twilight Sleep. New York: Appleton, 1927.

The Children. New York: Appleton, 1928.

Hudson River Bracketed. New York: Appleton, 1929.

Certain People. New York: Appleton, 1930.

The Gods Arrive. New York: Appleton, 1932.

Human Nature. New York: Appleton, 1933.

A Backward Glance. New York: Appleton-Century, 1934.

The World Over. New York: Appleton-Century, 1936.

Ghosts. New York: Appleton-Century, 1937. Stories from other volumes reprinted.
The Buccaneers. New York: Appleton-Century, 1938.

Short Stories (not included in the collections listed above)
"Mrs. Manstey's View." *Scribner's Magazine* 10, July, 1891.
"The Fulness of Life." *Scribner's Magazine* 14, December, 1893.
"That Good May Come." *Scribner's Magazine* 15, May, 1894.
"The Lamp of Psyche." *Scribner's Magazine* 18, October, 1895.
"The Valley of Childish Things and Other Emblems." *Century* 52, July, 1896.
"April Showers." *Youth's Companion* 74, January 18, 1900.
"Friends." *Youth's Companion* 74, August 23, 30, 1900.
"The Line of Least Resistance." *Lippincott's Magazine* 66, October, 1900.
"The House of the Dead Hand." *Atlantic Monthly* 94, August, 1904.
"The Introducers." *Ainslee's* 16, December, 1905, January, 1906.
"Les Metteurs en Scene." *Revue des Deux Mondes* 47, October, 1908. Never translated into English. Also in *Les Metteurs en Scene,* by Edith Wharton, Paris: Plon, Nourrit, 1909, selected stories translated into French by J. Chalençon et al.
"Writing a War Story." *Woman's Home Companion* 46, September, 1919.
"In a Day." *Woman's Home Companion* 60, January, February, 1933.

Articles (uncollected)
"The Three Francescas." *North American Review* 175, July, 1902.
"The Vice of Reading." *North American Review* 177, October, 1903.
"George Cabot Lodge." *Scribner's Magazine* 47, February, 1910.
"The Criticism of Fiction." *Times Literary Supplement,* May 14, 1914.

"Jean du Breuil de Saint-Germain." *Revue Hebdomadaire* 24, May 15, 1915.

"Les Français Vus par une Americaine. *Revue Hebdomadaire* 27, January 5, 1918.

"L'Amerique en Guerre. *Revue Hebdomadaire* 27, March 2, 1918.

"How Paris Welcomed the King." *Réveillé* 3, February 1919.

"Henry James in His Letters." *Quarterly Review* 234, July, 1920.

"Christmas Tinsel." *Delineator* 103, December, 1923.

"The Great American Novel." *Yale Review,* n.s. 16, July, 1927.

"William C. Brownell." *Scribner's Magazine* 84, November, 1928.

"A Cycle of Reviewing." *Spectator* 141, November 23, 1928.

"Visibility in Fiction." *Yale Review,* n.s. 18, March, 1929.

"Confessions of a Novelist." *Atlantic Monthly* 151, April, 1933.

"Tendencies in Modern Fiction." *Saturday Review of Literature* 10, January 27, 1934.

"Permanent Values in Fiction." *Saturday Review of Literature* 10, April 7, 1934.

"A Reconsideration of Proust." *Saturday Review of Literature* 11, October 27, 1934.

"Souvenirs du Bourget d'Outremer." *Revue Hebdomadaire* 45, June 21, 1936.

"A Little Girl's New York." *Harper's Magazine* 176, March, 1938.

Translation, Introductions, Etc.

The Joy of Living, by Hermann Sudermann, translated by Edith Wharton. New York: Scribner's, 1902.

A Village Romeo and Juliet, by Gottfried Keller, translated by Anna C. Bahlmann. Introduction by Edith Wharton. London: Constable, 1915.

The Book of the Homeless, edited by Edith Wharton. New York: Scribner's, 1916.

Futility, by William Gerhardi. Introduction by Edith Wharton. London: Cobden-Sanderson, 1922.

Bénédiction, by Claude Silve (Comtesse Philomène de Laforest-Divonne). Translated by Robert Norton. Foreword by Edith Wharton. New York: Appleton-Century, 1936.

Ethan Frome, a play by Owen and Donald Davis. Introduction by Edith Wharton. New York: Scribner's, 1936.

Eternal Passion in English Poetry, selected by Edith Wharton and Robert Norton, with the collaboration of Gaillard Lapsley. New York: Appleton-Century, 1939.

Reviews

Italian Cities, by Edwin H. and Evangeline W. Blashfield. *The Bookman* 12, August, 1901.

Ulysses, by Stephen Phillips. *Bookman* 15, April, 1902.

George Eliot, by Leslie Stephen. *Bookman* 15, May, 1902.

Belchamber, by Howard Sturgis. *Bookman* 21, May, 1905.

The Fool Errant, by Maurice Hewlett. *Bookman* 22, September, 1905.

The Sonnets of the Wingless Hours, by Eugene Lee-Hamilton. *The Bookman* 26, November, 1907.

Selections

An Edith Wharton Treasury, edited by Arthur H. Quinn. New York: Appleton-Century-Crofts, 1950.

Best Short Stories by Edith Wharton, edited by Wayne Andrews. New York: Scribner's, 1958. With biographical introduction, containing quotations from her papers.

II. Criticism, Memoirs, Background Studies, Etc.

The list is inevitably arbitrary, but all items are believed to illuminate Edith Wharton's work in some respect. Many additions could be made, particularly from references in *A Backward Glance.* There have been numerous other articles in periodicals, especially since this book first appeared.

Adams, Henry. *Mont St. Michel and Chartres.* London: Constable, 1936.

Auchincloss, Louis. "Edith Wharton and Her New Yorks." *Partisan Review* 18, July-August, 1951, and in *Reflections of a Jacobite.* Boston: Houghton Mifflin, 1961.

Auchincloss, Louis, *Edith Wharton.* Minneapolis: University of Minnesota Press, 1961.

Auchincloss, Louis. *Edith Wharton: A Woman in Her Time.* London: Michael Joseph, 1972.

Balsan, Consuelo Vanderbilt. *The Glitter & The Gold.* London: Heinemann, 1953.

Bell, Millicent. *Edith Wharton & Henry James.* London: Peter Owen, 1966.

Berenson, Bernard. *Sketch for a Self-Portrait.* London: Constable, 1949.

Bewley, Marius. *The Eccentric Design.* London: Chatto & Windus, 1959.

Blackmur, R. P. *The Lion and the Honeycomb.* London: Methuen, 1956.

Bourget, Paul. Introduction to *Chez les Heureux du Monde,* translated by C. du Bos. Paris: Plon, Nourrit, 1908.

Brooks, Van Wyck. *The Confident Years.* New York: Dutton, 1952.

Brown, E. K. *Edith Wharton: Etude Critique.* Paris: Librairie E. Droz, 1935.

Carroll, Loren. "Edith Wharton in Profile." *The Herald Tribune,* European Ed., 16 November, 1936.

Chase, Richard. *The American Novel and its Tradition.* London: G. Bell & Son, 1958.

Connolly, Cyril. *Les Pavillons.* London: H. Hamilton, 1962.

Cooper, Diana. *The Rainbow Comes and Goes.* London: Hart Davis, 1958.

Cowley, Malcolm. *Exile's Return.* London: Bodley, 1961.

Crosby, Caresse. *The Passionate Years.* New York: Dial Press, 1953.

Cunliffe, Marcus. *The Literature of the United States.* London: Penguin, 1954.

Davis, Lavinia. *A Bibliography of the Writings of Edith Wharton*. Portland, Maine: Southwood Press, 1933.

Downing, A. F. and Scully, V. J. *The Architectural Heritage of Newport, Rhode Island*. Cambridge: Harvard University Press, 1952.

Downing, A. J. *A Treatise on the Theory and Practice of Landscape Gardening, adapted to N. America*. New York: Putnam, 1849.

————. *The Architecture of Country Houses*. New York: D. Appleton and Company, 1853.

Edgell, G. H. *American Architecture To-day*. New York: Scribner's, 1928.

Edel, Leon. *Henry James: The Untried Years*. London: Hart Davis, 1953.

————. *Henry James: The Conquest of London*. London: Hart Davis, 1962.

————. *Henry James: The Middle Years*. London: Hart Davis, 1963.

————. *Henry James: The Treacherous Years*. London: Hart Davis, 1969.

————. *Henry James: The Master*. London: Hart Davis, 1972.

Hitchcock, Henry Russell. *Architecture in the Nineteenth & Twentieth Centuries*. London: Penguin, 1958.

Hoffman, Frederick J. *Points of Moral Reference: A Comparative Study of Edith Wharton & F. Scott Fitzgerald, English Institute Essays*. New York: Columbia University Press, 1950.

Howe, Irving, ed. *Edith Wharton*. New York: Prentice Hall, 1962.

James, Henry. *The American Scene* (including selected *Portraits of Places*), edited by W. H. Auden. New York: Scribner's, 1946.

————. *The Art of the Novel*. New York: Scribner's, 1934.

————. *Hawthorne*. London and New York: Macmillan, 1879.

————. *The Letters*, edited by Percy Lubbock. 2 vols. London: Macmillan, 1920.

————. *The Art of Fiction.* New York: Oxford University Press, 1948.

————. *Notebooks,* edited by F. O. Mathiessen & K. B. Murdock. New York: Oxford University Press, 1947.

Kazin, Alfred. *On Native Grounds.* New York: Reynal and Hitchcock, 1942.

Leavis, Q. D. "Henry James's Heiress: The Importance of Edith Wharton." *Scrutiny* 7, December, 1938.

Lehr, Elizabeth Drexel. *King Lehr and the Golden Age.* London: Constable, 1935.

Lewis, R. W. B. *Edith Wharton: A Biography.* London: Constable; New York: Harper and Row, 1975.

Lindberg, G. *Edith Wharton and the Novel of Manners.* Charlottesville: University Press of Virginia, 1975.

Lovett, Robert Morss. *Edith Wharton.* New York: McBride, 1925.

Lubbock, Percy. *The Craft of Fiction.* London: Jonathan Cape, 1921.

————. "The Novels of Edith Wharton." *Quarterly Review* 224, Jan., 1915.

————. *Portrait of Edith Wharton.* London: Jonathan Cape, 1947.

Lyde, Marilyn Jones. *Edith Wharton: Convention and Morality in the work of a Novelist.* Norman, Oklahoma: Oklahoma University Press, 1959.

Mansfield, Katherine. *Novels and Novelists,* edited by J. M. Murry. London: Constable, 1930.

Masson, Georgina. *Italian Gardens.* London: Thames & Hudson, 1961.

Mencken, H. L. *The American Language.* 4th ed. New York: Knopf, 1936.

Mizener, Arthur. *The Far Side of Paradise.* Boston: Houghton Mifflin, 1949.

Nevius, Blake. *Edith Wharton: A Study of her Fiction.* Berkeley: University of California Press, 1953.

Santayana, George. "The Genteel Tradition," *Winds of Doctrine.* New York: Scribner's, 1926.

Scott, Geoffrey. *The Architecture of Humanism*. London: Constable, 1947.

Sedgwick, Henry Dwight. *The New American Type and other Essays*. Boston: Houghton, Mifflin, 1908.

Sencourt, Robert. "The Poetry of Edith Wharton." *Bookman* 72, July, 1931.

Shepherd, J. C. and Jellicoe, G. A. *Italian Gardens of the Renaissance*. London: Tiranti, 1954.

Smith, Logan Pearsall. *Unforgotten Years*. London: Constable, 1938.

Trilling, Lionel. *The Liberal Imagination*. London: Secker & Warburg, 1951.

————. *A Gathering of Fugitives*. London: Secker & Warburg, 1957.

Underwood, John Curtis. *Literature and Insurgency: Ten Studies in Racial Evolution*. New York & London: Putnam, 1914.

Vanderbilt, Cornelius. *The Vanderbilt Feud*. London: Hutchinson, 1957.

Waldstein, Charles. "Social Ideals." *North American Review* 182, June, 1906; 183, July, 1906.

Wecter, Dixon. *The Saga of American Society*. New York: Scribner's, 1937.

Wilson, Edmund. *The Wound and the Bow*. London: Secker & Warburg, 1941.

————. *Classics and Commercials*. London: Secker & Warburg, 1950.

Winters, Ivor. "Maule's Curse." Reprinted in *In Defence of Reason*. London: Routledge, 1960.

Wolff, Cynthia Griffin. *A Feast of Words: The Triumph of Edith Wharton*. New York: Oxford University Press, 1977.

Index